PRACTICAL
HOLINESS

OTHER BOOKS AND MEDIA BY ALBERT HAASE, OFM

Swimming in the Sun:
  Rediscovering the Lord's Prayer with Francis of Assisi and Thomas Merton

Enkindled: Holy Spirit, Holy Gifts,
  coauthored with Bridget Haase, OSU

Instruments of Christ:
  Reflections on the Peace Prayer of St. Francis of Assisi

Coming Home to Your True Self:
  Leaving the Emptiness of False Attractions

Living the Lord's Prayer:
  The Way of the Disciple

The Lord's Prayer: A Summary of the Entire Gospel
  (Five CDs)

This Sacred Moment:
  Becoming Holy Right Where You Are

The Life of Antony of Egypt: by Athanasius,
  A Paraphrase

Catching Fire, Becoming Flame: A Guide for Spiritual Transformation

Catching Fire, Becoming Flame: A Guide for Spiritual Transformation
  (DVD/Video)

Keeping the Fire Alive: Navigating Challenges in the Spiritual Life
  (DVD/Video)

Come, Follow Me: Six Responses to the Call of Jesus
  (DVD/Video)

Saying Yes: Discovering and Responding to God's Will in Your Life

Saying Yes: What is God's Will for Me?
  (DVD/Video)

Becoming an Ordinary Mystic:
  Spirituality for the Rest of Us

ALBERT HAASE, OFM

PRACTICAL
HOLINESS

POPE FRANCIS
AS SPIRITUAL
COMPANION

PARACLETE PRESS
BREWSTER, MASSACHUSETTS

2019 First Printing

Practical Holiness: Pope Francis as Spiritual Companion

Copyright © 2019 Franciscan Friars of the State of Missouri

ISBN 978-1-64060-197-0

Library of Congress Cataloging-in-Publication Data is available.

10 9 8 7 6 5 4 3 2 1

Published by Paraclete Press
Brewster, Massachusetts

Printed in the United States of America

"My modest goal is to repropose
the call to holiness in a practical
way for our own time, with
all its risks, challenges and
opportunities" (2).

POPE FRANCIS,
Gaudete et Exsultate

CONTENTS

INTRODUCTION   1

CHAPTER 1
The Call to Holiness   5

CHAPTER 2
Two Subtle Enemies of Holiness   27

CHAPTER 3
In the Light of the Master   45

CHAPTER 4
Signs of Holiness in Today's World   73

CHAPTER 5
Spiritual Combat, Vigilance,
and Discernment   118

CONCLUSION   151

APPENDIX 1
What's Next?   153

APPENDIX 2
Forty Questions for Forty Days   157

Introduction

Pope Francis is sending a message, I thought to myself. An archbishop, not a cardinal, and two laypeople led the press conference.

On Monday, April 9, 2018, at 12:15pm, Archbishop Angelo De Donatis, the pope's Vicar of Rome, Paola Bignardi, head of the widespread lay movement *Azione Cattolica*, and Gianni Valente, a well-known Italian journalist and personal friend of Pope Francis, presented to the universal Church *Gaudete et Exsultate*, the pope's apostolic exhortation on holiness in the contemporary world. The fact that not a single official from any Vatican office was present intensified the pope's nonverbal message: this document was not meant for spiritual elites but for the ordinary person in the pew.

I was preaching in St. John's, Newfoundland, when *Rejoice and Be Glad: On Holiness in the Contemporary World*, its English title, was released. Less than an hour later, I downloaded the text and began to read it. With each paragraph, a wave of enthusiasm washed over me. I quickly realized this text was the advice of a wise spiritual director or companion (I use the words interchangeably) who wanted to highlight "the risks, challenges and opportunities" (2) we all face in fulfilling our vocation to become saints.

As a spiritual director and trainer of spiritual directors, I am constantly on the lookout for wise, practical guidance in all matters spiritual. In this apostolic exhortation, Pope Francis offers us just that, and more. He highlights not only the pitfalls and challenges of the spiritual life, but also those moments when, unbeknownst to us, grace is offered. More than a pep talk to continue the spiritual journey, *Gaudete et Exsultate* is a compendium of astute advice and down-to-earth spirituality offered by an eighty-one-year-old spiritual director who just so happens to be the 266th pontiff of the Roman Catholic Church.

Practical Holiness: Pope Francis as Spiritual Companion contains my thoughts, reflections, and musings on this apostolic exhortation. Pope Francis is not the tightest of writers—sometimes a paragraph reads more like a stream of consciousness with a word association connecting one sentence to the next. I'll present his wisdom in a more direct and understandable way. In one place he uses a Greek word, and in two other places English words I had to look up in the dictionary. Don't worry—I'll help you with his meaning. I'll tell you a little about the saints he mentions in passing and assumes we know. I'll share with you my reactions and some stories that the text brought to mind. When I quote the text, I indicate the paragraph number in parentheses; when my paragraph includes multiple quotes from the same numbered paragraph of the apostolic exhortation, I indicate the paragraph number only in the last quote. My five chapter titles mirror those of the exhortation. When I introduce you to my spiritual directees and friends, please know I've changed their names and circumstances to protect their privacy.

As you read this book, I hope you will be motivated to get a copy of *Gaudete et Exsultate* and reflect upon it for yourself. There are several good printed editions available. You can also download a free copy at http://w2.vatican.va/content/francesco/en/apost_exhortations/documents/papa-francesco_esortazione-ap_20180319_gaudete-et-exsultate.html. You'll discover the wisdom of a holy and practical man. You'll also discover that Pope Francis is no nonchalant tourist to otherworldly realms but an experienced companion for the spiritual journey. His GPS tracker to holiness, firmly rooted in Scripture and Christian tradition, does not take us down secret, difficult passageways and up narrow, rarefied peaks requiring spiritual Sherpas with superhuman skills and esoteric knowledge. Instead, his GPS simply indicates our current location and gives us the time-honored directions used by all the saints: find your own unique way of living the practical challenges of the Beatitudes right here, right now.

ALBERT HAASE, OFM
Feast of All Saints

CHAPTER 1
The Call to Holiness

On a chilly afternoon and twenty minutes early for her first spiritual direction appointment, Beverly arrived, nervously clutching a spent Kleenex as she patted beads of perspiration on her forehead.

Eager, nervous, or scared? I didn't know.

We sat down. She blurted out, "My life is a mess."

Discouraged or maybe depressed. "I beg your pardon?"

"My life is a mess. I just don't know where to begin. I look over the past fifty years. I wonder how I got here."

The cadence suggests this is from the introduction she prepared in her head. I didn't have to wait long for her to start ad-libbing.

"I've always wanted to be an example of what it means to be a good Christian but I made a shipwreck of my life. Twenty years ago, I nagged my husband right out of the door and subsequently divorced him. I was left with two children to raise and no job skills. My ex's child support was spotty. I hustled to get two jobs—at a fast food restaurant and cleaning houses on the weekends—because I needed to put food on the table and wanted my sons to live comfortably. I sacrificed for them, brought them to their baseball games and church, and did the best I could so they would become fine men with strong Christian values. I hope I succeeded.

"But in raising my boys and working two jobs, I often forgot to pray. I told God that I would have to catch him in the car or during my lunch breaks. Well, I didn't do either often. I just celebrated my fiftieth birthday and told myself it was time to get serious about my relationship with God.

"But I'm afraid I might have waited too long and wonder if God is even interested in me now. When I look at my life, I know I can't be like Mother Teresa and dedicate myself to the poor on the streets. That just isn't my cup of tea. And I'll certainly never be like Saint Teresa of Avila and have a mystical prayer life because I haven't prayed enough. I know a little bit about St. Thérèse of Lisieux's little way of love and I think I might be able to live that. I just need to learn how to do it.

"So, here I am, Father, at age fifty. I want to begin spiritual direction and try to make up for lost time in the spiritual life. What should I do?"

That was ten years ago, and I still remember being touched by Beverly's brutal honesty and spiritual hunger. I also stand in awe of what she has discovered over the past decade: without even knowing it, she had been on a spiritual path, and the "mess" of her life had been drenched in the grace of God.

The Example of the Saints

Beverly is surprised, encouraged, and challenged by what Pope Francis says in his apostolic exhortation. He states emphatically, at the very beginning of the document, that God calls each one of us to be holy. That includes divorced Beverly who once thought she might have been unworthy of a relationship with God.

Throughout the document, the pope highlights important figures in Scripture and in our spiritual tradition who blossomed into holy, saintly people. Referring to the eleventh chapter of the Letter to the Hebrews, he mentions Abraham and Sarah, who, elderly as they were, left their home and followed the call of God; Moses, who, following the call of God, led the Israelites from slavery to freedom; and Gideon, who, as a leader of the Israelites and at great disadvantage with a small army, won a decisive battle against the Midianites.

Besides an elderly couple, an appointed leader, and a soldier, Pope Francis also refers to and quotes some famous and not-so-famous beatified and canonized saints:

- Blessed Maria Gabriella Sagheddu, a Trappistine nun who offered her life as a spiritual sacrifice for the cause of Christian unity;
- Philip Neri, known for his playful sense of humor and shrewd wit, whose piety was distinguished by a practical ordinariness;
- Francis of Assisi, the famous saint of contemporary suburban birdbaths, who followed in the footsteps of Christ by imitating the Gospel life literally;
- Bernard of Clairvaux, who reinvigorated the Benedictine life and highlighted the importance of emotions in one's prayer life;
- Bonaventure, the medieval Franciscan theologian and official biographer of Saint Francis;
- Francis de Sales, who wrote the first handbook of lay spirituality;
- Thomas Aquinas, the medieval theologian who wrote the most influential synthesis of Christian theology;
- Teresa Benedicta of the Cross, who was a German Jewish philosopher, converted to Catholicism, and was martyred as a Carmelite nun;
- Mother Teresa of Calcutta, the saint of India's slums who ministered to the poorest of the poor;
- John of the Cross, the great Carmelite mystic of the sixteenth century;

- Ignatius Loyola, the founder of the Jesuits, whose spirituality is based on "finding God in all things";
- Josephine Bakhita, a former slave from the Sudan who became a Canossian sister, ministering in Italy for forty-five years;
- John Paul II, who emphasized the universal call to holiness and beatified 1,340 people and canonized 483 people, more than the combined tally of all pontiffs in the preceding five centuries.

Added to these saints, Pope Francis makes special reference to the "genius of women" whose attractiveness is "an essential means of reflecting God's holiness in the world" (12). Some of the women mentioned are these:

- Hildegard of Bingen, the twelfth-century German Benedictine abbess, writer, composer, philosopher, Christian mystic, and visionary who was declared a Doctor of the Church in 2012;
- Bridget, the married mother of eight children who, starting from age seven, had visions of the crucified Christ;
- Catherine of Siena, a tertiary of the Dominican Order and future Doctor of the Church, whose influence upon the papacy played a role in the return of the Pope from Avignon to Rome during the Great Schism of the West;

- Teresa of Avila, the sixteenth-century Carmelite mystic and reformer of the Carmelite Order;
- Thérèse of Lisieux, the popular "Little Flower," who believed that ordinary actions done with love became extraordinary.

The pope also makes passing reference to "those unknown or forgotten women who, each in her own way, sustained and transformed families and communities by the power of their witness" (12).

Ordinary People, Extraordinary Lives

It would be somewhat disconcerting if *Gaudete et Exsultate* only mentioned these past spiritual giants as witnesses to God's grace and models of holiness. We could easily find ourselves sharing in Beverly's discouragement and inability to imitate Mother Teresa of Calcutta and Teresa of Avila. But in a wonderful appreciation for God's abundant grace transforming the most ordinary of people, the document also includes "our own mothers, grandmothers or other loved ones." And with a nod to holiness being neither instantaneous nor healing us of our weaknesses, Pope Francis states, "Their lives may not always have been perfect, yet even amid their faults and failings they kept moving forward and proved pleasing to the Lord" (3). Holiness is something that gradually happens to us, one step forward and two steps back, but doesn't necessarily remove our character flaws: Saint Jerome struggled with anger and its accompanying remorse until the day he died, and Saint Alphonsus Liguori, a Doctor of the Church, battled with an excessive fear of having offended God and committed sin.

Though we might think of the canonized saints as the upper class of holiness, the pontiff borrows an expression from a French author, Joseph Malègue, and speaks of "the middle class of holiness" (7). He speaks of our next-door neighbors who reflect God's presence in our midst. These are the silent, unsung heroes of holiness who witness to the Spirit's fruit of patience: parents like Beverly who work two jobs for their children; those who patiently endure sickness in hospitals; and elderly religious nuns and sisters who continue to smile.

I instantly thought of my own mother who, widowed at age forty-eight by my father's suicide, was challenged to enter the workforce after being a stay-at-home mother with only a high school education. I have distinct memories of her eating peanut butter and jelly sandwiches while she served steak and potatoes to my two brothers and me. I thought of my maternal grandmother who went out of her way not only to help support my mother financially but also to encourage her daily in the challenges she faced. Though both were terribly flawed and probably will never be officially canonized, my mother and grandmother reflected God's sacrificial love lived by people throughout the world.

The pope also makes clear that holiness is not confined to the Catholic Church. Quoting John Paul II, he notes how "the Holy Spirit raises up 'signs of his presence which help Christ's followers'" (9) outside the Catholic Church and in different contexts: for example, martyrs for the faith—Catholics, Orthodox Christians, Anglicans, and Protestants—who witness to the unity already shared by the Christian community.

As the People of God, we form a vibrant community of faith. We need one another. We encourage one another. We challenge one another. We help each other blossom into the person God has called us to be. "That is why no one is saved alone, as an isolated individual" (6). Holiness is a family affair.

Brother John the Simple

We all know canonized and saintly individuals—and the temptation to try and imitate them. Like Beverly, we cross off our list those whom we could never emulate and narrow our search for the ones who offer us a doable model, in the hope of getting into heaven by hanging on to their coattails.

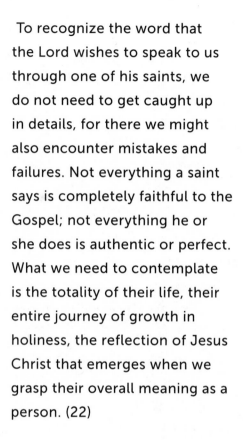

To recognize the word that the Lord wishes to speak to us through one of his saints, we do not need to get caught up in details, for there we might also encounter mistakes and failures. Not everything a saint says is completely faithful to the Gospel; not everything he or she does is authentic or perfect. What we need to contemplate is the totality of their life, their entire journey of growth in holiness, the reflection of Jesus Christ that emerges when we grasp their overall meaning as a person. (22)

There's a story from my Franciscan tradition that illustrates this. Brother John was a simple man who wanted to follow Saint Francis perfectly. He scrupulously watched Francis in church in order to copy the saint's actions. If he saw the saint genuflecting or raising his hands in prayer, Brother John would do the same. If he heard Francis spit or cough, Brother John would spit or cough. Brother John was playacting, and Francis, who loved simplicity in people and had a profound appreciation and respect for each friar's individuality, reprimanded Brother John. Holiness is not attained by mere behavior modification or wearing a costume; it's about putting on the "new self" (Eph. 4:24), the true you.

Your Own Call to Holiness

In order to avoid that naïve, childish, and cookie-cutter understanding of how to become a saint, Pope Francis quotes Vatican II's universal call to holiness—". . . all the faithful, whatever their condition or state, are called by the Lord—each in his or her own way—to that perfect holiness by which the Father himself is perfect" (10). He then continues: "There are some testimonies that may prove helpful and inspiring, but that we are not meant to copy, for that could even lead us astray from the one specific path that the Lord has in mind for us. The important thing is that each believer discern his or her own path, that they bring out the very best of themselves, the most personal gifts that God has placed in their hearts (cf. 1 *Cor.* 12:7), rather than hopelessly trying to imitate something not meant for them. We are all called to be witnesses, but there are many actual ways of bearing witness" (11).

Over the past ten years, that's what Beverly has been discovering. Though she admires Thérèse of Lisieux and is inspired by her simple way of life, Beverly has gradually realized and accepted the challenge of practical holiness before her. "God already has one Little Flower from France. He doesn't want another. What he now wants is one Beverly from Dallas."

Here's another vignette from my Franciscan tradition. As he lay dying, Saint Francis was asked to describe the perfect friar. No doubt surprising the friars, the saint replied that the perfect friar had Brother Bernard's faith and love of poverty, Brother Leo's simplicity and purity, the courtesy and kindness of Brother Angelo, Brother Masseo's gracious look and natural good sense, the prayerfulness of Brothers Giles and Rufino, Brother Juniper's patience and desire to follow the crucified Christ, the bodily and spiritual courage of Brother John of Lauds, the charity of Brother Roger, and the love of itinerancy of Brother Lucidus, who was unwilling to remain in any place longer than a month.

Though each and every friar had professed to follow in the footsteps of Jesus Christ, Francis's reply indicates that each one did it in his own way. Each had his own unique path that brought out the best in himself and witnessed to the multifaceted beauty of a Franciscan vocation.

This is the challenge of *Rejoice and Be Glad*. We are reminded on virtually every page of chapter one that there is no one-size-fits-all or cookie-cutter approach to sanctity. Whether you are male, female, married, vowed, single, straight, gay, a painter, paralegal, paramedic, pastry chef, politician, pediatrician, pharmacist, photographer, police officer, or postal worker, you have the challenge of discovering your unique path of being a witness and reflection of God's presence in the world.

Your Path, Your Mission

Your unique path of witnessing and reflecting God's presence is really your personal mission. Speaking to each one of us, Pope Francis writes, "Each saint is a mission, planned by the Father to reflect and embody, at a specific moment in history, a certain aspect of the Gospel" (19). Later he writes, "Every saint is a message which the Holy Spirit takes from the riches of Jesus Christ and gives to his people" (21). Consequently, this mission is experienced in union with Christ and is stamped with the mysteries of his life, particularly his death and resurrection; it's our commitment to build with Jesus the kingdom of peace, love, and justice.

This is a powerful summons to all of us. You too need to see the entirety of your life as a mission. Try to do so by listening to God in prayer and recognizing the signs that he gives you. Always ask the Spirit what Jesus expects from you at every moment of your life and in every decision you must make, so as to discern its place in the mission you have received. Allow the Spirit to forge in you the personal mystery that can reflect Jesus Christ in today's world. (23)

Don't confuse your God-given mission with your occupation as a webmaster, waitress, welder, or writer; don't mistaken it with your role as spouse, parent, lover, or friend. It's so much more than an occupation or role. Your mission is to reflect Jesus to the world, to help build his kingdom, and to uniquely live out the Gospel and the God-spoken message of your life as you cut the customer's hair, help someone choose a retirement plan, or empty the dishwasher. Mission and message are about kingdom building and baptismal passion.

Looking to Jesus

Pope Francis offers us a practical way to incarnate Jesus's life in our choices and attitudes. Influenced by his Jesuit tradition, he proposes the contemplation of Jesus's life as taught and practiced by Ignatius of Loyola.

You might not be familiar with the Ignatian approach to praying with the life of Jesus. Here's a simple way to do it:

1. Get comfortable in a chair. Take a few deep breaths. Call to mind that you are in the presence of God.
2. Choose a scene from the Gospel. Prayerfully read the passage for the details of the story. Pause and ponder it. Read it a second and third time.
3. Close your eyes and slowly relive the entire scene in your imagination. Imagine the weather as well as the site, sounds, and smells of the story. Place yourself in the story and engage it intellectually and emotionally. Perhaps you are one of the main characters—the paralytic, the woman caught in adultery, the older brother of the Prodigal Son, the man born blind—or perhaps you are one of the bystanders.
4. As you mentally reenact the entire scene and hear the words of Jesus and of the bystanders, note your thoughts, feelings, and reactions.

5. After you have relived the story with its dialogue slowly and deliberately, ask yourself three questions:

   • What does this story say to my head? What information do I receive about God, Jesus, or the Spirit from this Gospel scene?

   • What does this story say to my heart? What feelings and emotions does it elicit?

   • What does this story say to my hands? How am I called to uniquely live out the message of this story in my daily life?

6. Conclude with a prayer of commitment to Jesus and a prayer of thanksgiving for discovering another aspect of the message God wants to speak through you to the world.

Different Yet the Same

Though each one of us has a unique path to sanctity and a singular way of helping Jesus build the kingdom, Pope Francis makes clear our universal challenge and vocation: "We are called to be holy by living our lives with love and by bearing witness in everything we do, wherever we find ourselves" (14). He quotes Pope Benedict XVI, "[H]oliness is nothing other than charity lived to the full" (21). Holiness is love enfleshed.

Unfortunately, many people think that kind of love requires audacious actions and dramatic decisions. That was my youthful misunderstanding. I thought I could become a saint by flying to the other side of the world and spending more than eleven years as a missionary to mainland China.

The pope offers us a practical corrective to that misunderstanding. Following a woman during one of her typical days, he highlights how incremental steps to holiness are offered in small, loving actions: her refusal to spread gossip; the time she spent listening to her child's hopes and dreams even though she herself was weary and tired; her faith-filled prayer in the midst of anxiety; her offer of a kind word to a poor person on the street.

The pontiff goes on to note how the great challenges of life are times when God calls us to a renewed conversion to witness to his grace or to discover a more perfect way of doing what we are doing. He repeats the wisdom of the late Cardinal Francis-Xavier Nguyễn Văn Thuận, who was detained by the communist government of Vietnam in a reeducation camp for thirteen years, nine in solitary confinement. Instead of waiting for some future day to be set free, the cardinal chose "to live in the present moment, filling it to the brim with love" (17). Upon reading that, I immediately thought of Jesus's statement that the world will know we are his disciples by our love (see John 13:35), Augustine of Hippo's famous statement, "Love and do what you will," and John of the Cross's reminder

that "When evening comes, you will be examined in love."
Loving gestures, no matter how small they might be, are
ways to build the kingdom and give witness to our mission
and vocation "as good stewards of the manifold grace of
God (*1 Pet.* 4:10)" (18).

Two Exemplars
You May Not Yet Know

Two good stewards of God's manifold grace of love
were home-grown right here in the United States: Julia
Greeley and Stanley Rother.

Born sometime between 1833 and 1848 in Hannibal,
Missouri, Julia Greeley was freed from slavery by
Missouri's Emancipation Act of 1865. She traveled to
Wyoming, New Mexico, and Colorado as she served
as housekeeper and nanny to white families. Baptized
a Roman Catholic in 1880 at Sacred Heart Church in
Denver, she quickly developed a strong devotion to the
Sacred Heart of Jesus. This devotion fueled her love for
the poor and for firefighters. Denver's "Angel of Mercy,"
with crippling arthritis, would spend her nights pulling a
little red wagon and distributing to the needy everyday
necessities purchased with her ten-dollar monthly salary.
She did her acts of charity always under cover of night, so
people wouldn't be embarrassed being helped by a black
woman. She expressed her compassion for firefighters

by traveling on foot every month to Denver's firehouses, where she delivered Sacred Heart devotional materials. She died on June 7, 1918, the feast of the Sacred Heart of Jesus, and more than a thousand people attended her funeral. Her Cause for Canonization was officially opened in December 2016.

Raised on a farm, Stanley Rother was ordained a priest for the Archdiocese of Oklahoma City in 1963. After three parish assignments as associate pastor, his request to serve the archdiocesan foreign mission in the rural highlands of southwest Guatemala was granted. He ministered there until his death in 1981. His willingness to do physical labor and keep an open-door policy at his rectory endeared him to the Tz'utujil people (a Native American people of the Maya ethnic group) whom he served. Though he had flunked out of his first seminary because he was unable to learn Latin, within five years he was not only preaching and celebrating the Mass in the local language but also translating the New Testament into Tz'utujil. By 1980, his parishioners and catechists were disappearing, being beaten, and tortured to death by the government. Warned that he was number eight on a death list and advised to leave in January 1981, he reluctantly went back to Oklahoma. Within three months, he wanted to return to his parishioners and celebrate Easter. So he asked and received the bishop's permission to return to his mission—even though he knew it would mean his death.

His oldest brother, Tom, told me Stanley had told him, "A shepherd cannot run from his flock." On the morning of July 28, just after midnight, gunmen entered his rectory, found him, and shot this faithful pastor twice in the head. Rother was beatified as the first American martyr on September 23, 2017, at Oklahoma City's Cox Convention Center, with approximately 20,000 people in attendance.

Greeley and Rother couldn't be any more different: a nineteenth-century black woman who converted to Catholicism, a twentieth-century white priest who was a missionary. Yet each fulfilled the common vocation of sacrificial love, the hallmark of holiness, in a unique way. Julia, like the poor widow in the Gospel (see Lk. 21:1–4), shared the little she had with others; Stanley, like the Good Shepherd (see John 10:11), gave his life for his flock. They each had their eyes on Jesus and helped him to build the kingdom by living the particular message God wanted to speak through their lives.

Holding the Tension

Remember how Beverly said with some regret that she told God she would have to catch him in the car or during her lunch breaks? She thought her life was less than laudatory because, caught up in raising her sons and holding down two jobs, she couldn't find a specific, dedicated time to sit down and pray.

We need a spirit of holiness capable of filling both our solitude and our service, our personal life and our evangelizing efforts, so that every moment can be an expression of self-sacrificing love in the Lord's eyes. In this way, every minute of our lives can be a step along the path to growth in holiness. (31)

Some young clergy and vowed religious have a similar mindset. They become bothered when a parishioner interrupts them and asks for some advice, to go to confession, or to have a sick relative anointed. They refuse to take important phone calls during prayer. As a newly ordained priest once told me, "Nothing is more important than my time with God," seemingly suggesting that God cannot be found in the midst of ministry. These people "relegate pastoral engagement or commitment in the world to second place, as if these were 'distractions' along the path to growth in holiness and interior peace" (27).

Pope Francis wisely reminds us to embrace the tension between prayer and service, solitude and activity. He bluntly states, "Everything can be accepted and integrated into our life in this world, and become a part of our path to holiness" (26). Practical holiness entails juggling time for prayer and personal leisure with our responsibilities and commitments—and knowing that sometimes one must give way to the other.

Juggling prayer with work and finding the balance are not easy. They require listening to both the promptings of our hearts and the tension and stress of our physical bodies. The Benedictine motto *Ora et Labora*, "Prayer and Work," reminds us that an overabundance of prayer and leisure can lead to idleness and a bogus spirituality; an overabundance of activity and ministry can lead to resentment and burnout. The path to holiness creatively cuts through the middle of that tension.

Chapter one of the apostolic exhortation ends with a quote from the late nineteenth- and early twentieth-century novelist and essayist Léon Bloy: "The only great tragedy in life is not to become a saint" (34). In light of what the pontiff has written, that quote takes on a deeper meaning and offers a greater challenge than I had initially thought. My sanctity is not a matter of pretending to be another Francis of Assisi and renouncing my possessions, imitating Teresa of Avila and prepping for mystical prayer, or following Uncle Charlie and becoming a daily volunteer at a soup kitchen. It's about discovering my unique and singular mission of helping Jesus make the kingdom of love, peace, and justice a reality at this specific moment in history. It's about becoming the message of enfleshed love that God from all eternity wanted to speak to the world when he created me.

REFLECTION QUESTIONS

1. Think of a relative or friend, living or deceased, whom you consider a saint. Why do you consider this person holy? What was the message God wanted to speak to you through his or her life?

2. How did you reflect Jesus and help him build the kingdom yesterday?

3. What's more enticing to you: prayer or work? Think back to a time when you lost a healthy balance between the two. How did you know you were off balance and how did you get back on track?

CHAPTER 2

Two Subtle Enemies of Holiness

I've been training future spiritual directors for ten years. It's the favorite part of my ministry, and it presents unique responsibilities and challenges.

Someone prepared for the ministry of spiritual direction needs to know the spiritual tradition and the mine of wisdom imbedded in it. Both offer important signposts and landmarks along the spiritual journey.

A trained spiritual director or companion must also have a profound respect for a person's conscience. John Henry Newman called it "the aboriginal Vicar of Christ." A companion must never violate it with loose lips or impossible impositions.

Spiritual companions also need to be trained in basic listening and feedback skills. The classic portrait of a spiritual companion with a very small mouth and big, floppy ears speaks volumes about the stance of a good listener who is hesitant to offer advice or instruction. A well-trained director, when speaking, will ask more open-ended questions than give guidance. He or she helps direct the person's attention to the Holy Spirit's call and action. A good spiritual companion does not direct or take charge of a life. Know-it-alls haven't fared well in my training program.

Another major challenge for any spiritual director or companion, either novice or experienced, is allowing God to be God in the person's life. Novice spiritual directors are prone to fix a person's problem, highlight a questionable behavior, or quickly tell the person how to think, feel, or act. Like personal trainers, novice directors will sometimes tell the people they are companioning about certain spiritual practices and prayer techniques they should be using—but this suggests that spiritual progress is the result of brute will power. I like to warn future spiritual directors, "If you find yourself overthinking, doing all the talking, offering specific strategies, or working too hard to find a solution during a session, you're probably out of your field and playing amateur counselor or life coach. Let the Spirit guide the person according to God's timetable."

As I read chapter two of *Rejoice and Be Glad*, I began to wish I could bring Pope Francis in as a guest lecturer for my training course. I'd have him teach every single lesson, in fact, but I know he doesn't have the time! The pope highlights two heresies—one offering doctrinal, the other disciplinary, security—that can be tempting and attractive to spiritual directors as they sit with people eager for spiritual growth. The first is overly concerned with thought (theological analysis and intellectual classification) while the second with action (inspection and verification of proper behavior). Both shut the door of the heart to the transforming presence of God. Let the buyer beware: Not every spiritual director or companion is good for the soul. John of the Cross goes one step farther and says a spiritual companion can sometimes even be an obstacle to a person's spiritual growth.

Gnosticism

The first heresy is Gnosticism, which emphasizes a subjective faith only interested "in a certain experience or a set of ideas and bits of information which are meant to console and enlighten" (36).

I couldn't help thinking of my spiritual director from my college seminary days during the 1970s in southern Illinois. The charismatic renewal was quite popular at the time, and my spiritual director was one of the leaders of a local prayer group. It was evident that charismatic prayer had reinvigorated his spiritual life. "Albert," he would pressure me, "you must make a Life in the Spirit Seminar and be baptized in the Holy Spirit. That will show people you are serious about the spiritual life." He had clearly unlocked the secret to spiritual growth—for himself and for me. For this priest, baptism in the Holy Spirit was the only true sign of Christian commitment.

In my own personal prayer life, I have found the Ignatian Daily Examen, a prayerful review of the day when one rummages for the presence of God in the mundane details of daily living, extraordinarily helpful, satisfying, and challenging. My zeal for the technique sometimes spills over in my spiritual direction sessions as I prod a directee to try it for thirty days. Enthusiasm for such spiritual experiences as baptism in the Holy Spirit or a Cursillo retreat, a prayer technique like the Examen or the Divine Mercy chaplet, or even induction into the Knights of Columbus is admirable; the Gnostic, however, canonizes it as the be-all and end-all of spiritual formation.

Just as attractive are information and knowledge that know-it-alls think explain everything, both spiritual and theological. These Gnostics are imprisoned in their heads by an "encyclopedia of abstractions" (37) and mistakenly think they have cracked the code for all theological discussions and scriptural interpretations. They neatly wrap the Gospel and the faith in an attractive box of logic and understanding. But beware: Gnostics, rigid and narrow-minded, want to dominate everything with their pet theories and pat answers.

I have met professors of theology and teachers of Christian spiritual formation who have fallen prey to this false form of holiness. The pontiff, indicating just how subtle it can be, notes, "When somebody has an answer for every question, it is a sign that they are not on the right road" (41). Overly talkative spiritual companions who quickly and easily dollop advice like a spiritual Ann Landers do well to take another look at their attitudes and examine their beliefs.

Why is Gnosticism not only a false form of holiness but also a dangerous deviation from orthodoxy? Because it tries to control God, "to domesticate the mystery, whether the mystery of God and his grace, or the mystery of others' lives" (40). God and divine action—grace—are ineffable and can never be coaxed, contained, or explained. Our minds short-circuit and our words wobble, stumble, and fall when trying to accurately describe the divine reality. St. Augustine is famous for saying, "If you understand it, it's not God." We cannot control God or conjure up a divine encounter with the snap of a finger or a wave of a wand. "God infinitely transcends us; he is full of surprises" (41).

> Nor can we claim to say where God is not, because God is mysteriously present in the life of every person, in a way that he himself chooses, and we cannot exclude this by our presumed certainties. Even when someone's life appears completely wrecked, even when we see it devastated by vices or addictions, God is present there. If we let ourselves be guided by the Spirit rather than our own preconceptions, we can and must try to find the Lord in every human life. This is part of the mystery that a gnostic mentality cannot accept, since it is beyond its control. (42)

Pope Francis, after noting the mystery of God, acknowledges the mystery of every person's life. What does he mean by that? Though he doesn't explain it, I suspect it could be the mystery, for example, apparent in our identity and self-awareness. We are not born with complete self-knowledge. We grow into the mystery of our identity as we journey through childhood, adolescence, adulthood, and old age. That journey involves discovery through experimentation and trial by error. For many of us, it is an arduous, evolving, and sometimes confusing journey. I now know more about myself in my sixties than I did when I was twenty-one. A sacred self-revelation and identity flower as we maneuver through life and walk through various terrains that elicit validating, questionable, and sometimes sinful behavior.

Gnostics can hear none of this. They hold children and adolescents to the exact same moral standards as adults and senior citizens. There is no room for questions, gray areas, or an evolving self-identity. All behavior is either black or white, sinful or righteous. Gnostics often nitpick over sexual morality and consider themselves enlightened when it comes to normative behavior. They know where God's grace flourishes and where it falters.

This presents a challenge for every spiritual director or companion, both novice and seasoned. To sit with an unmarried directee who is involved in a committed sexual relationship or struggling with some recurring vice or addiction can be both unsettling and uncomfortable. The temptation arises to fix, judge, and maybe even reprimand people who are stuck in compromised situations—in other words, to accuse them of slamming shut the door to grace. But God is present everywhere and in every situation and in every person. The role of the spiritual director is not to manage and direct another's life; it is to direct the person's *attention* to God's continual invitation to open the door of the heart wider and wider.

Gnosticism versus Mysticism

After a small group of eleven followers had gathered around Francis of Assisi, the future saint decided to go to Rome and seek permission from the Pope to live "the Gospel life" of radical poverty and itinerancy. There was discussion and dispute as the Roman pontiff and cardinals struggled with such a novel idea. When one cardinal—clearly whom *Gaudete et Exsultate* would label a Gnostic—said that such a lifestyle was impossible, the cardinal supporting Francis and his followers replied, "If we say what he seeks to do is impossible, we are saying to live the Gospel entrusted to us by Jesus Christ is impossible! All this penitent from Assisi wants, is to live what we are called to live!" After further discussion, the pope blessed Francis's intentions.

The story highlights not only how Gnosticism, scorning "the concrete simplicity of the Gospel" (43), can restrict the Holy Spirit but also how it comes into conflict with mysticism. There is a spiritual continuum with the institutional Gnostic at one end and the Spirit-led mystic at the other end. Some people rigidly stand at one end of the spectrum and consequently challenge and clash with the opposite end—as did the two cardinals in the early life of St. Francis. And yet, we need them both. To ignore the Gnostic is to walk a slippery slope where preposterous thoughts and irrational feelings might dominate and steer one's life. To ignore the mystic is to fall prey to the temptation and delusion that we have figured out the mind of God and trapped divine grace in a box. Those who are spiritually mature, and experienced directors or companions, respect both endpoints yet still allow God to be God in their own lives and in the lives of others.

Don't get the impression that Pope Francis's criticism of Gnosticism suggests he is an anti-intellectual. Far from it. He clearly promotes theological study as long as it does not water down the Christian experience to "a set of intellectual exercises that distance us from the freshness of the Gospel" (46). Quoting his saintly namesake's advice to St. Anthony of Padua, who asked if it was proper for a theologian in the Franciscan Order to teach, the saint from Assisi approved, "provided that . . . you do not extinguish the spirit of prayer and devotion during study of this kind" (46). The wisdom that comes from theological study must never be separated from the Gospel mandate requiring "mercy towards our neighbor" (46) or "touching Christ's suffering flesh in others" (37). The goal of theological study, like the goal of the spiritual life, is love. Sadly, with the Gnostic, theory triumphs over tenderness.

Pelagianism

Unlike Gnosticism, which canonizes the ability of the intellect, Pelagianism lionizes the human will and personal effort. It pushes God and divine grace off their pedestals and replaces them with laws, programs, and techniques.

The Church has repeatedly taught that we are justified not by our own works or efforts, but by the grace of the Lord, who always takes the initiative. (52)

The Pelagians are spiritual athletes who believe that all holiness is man-made. They trust in their own powers, flaunting their superiority "because they observe certain rules or remain intransigently faithful to a particular Catholic style" (49). Paragraph 57 of the apostolic exhortation specifies their contemporary fixations and preoccupations:

- *An obsession with the law*: No doubt with the best of intentions, present-day Pelagians are like the Pharisees of Jesus's day who consistently gave priority to obedience over love, mercy, and compassion. These contemporary Pharisees believe that dotting every i and crossing every t of even the most insignificant regulation not only shows one's religious devotion but also makes one holy. They forget the most basic Pauline insight: "Owe no one anything, except to love one another; for the one who loves another has fulfilled the law. The commandments, 'You shall not commit adultery; You shall not murder; You shall not steal; You shall not covet'; and any other commandment, are summed up in this word, 'Love your neighbor as yourself.' Love does no wrong to a neighbor; therefore, love is the fulfilling of the law" (Rom. 3:8–10). And again, "For the whole law is summed up in a single commandment, 'You shall love your neighbor as yourself'" (Gal. 5:14).

- *An absorption with social and political advantages*: Pelagians and spiritual athletes enjoy the social status and snob value that come with appearing religiously and morally perfect. Think of Jesus's criticism of the scribes and Pharisees: "They do all their deeds to be seen by others; for they make their phylacteries broad and their fringes long. They love to have the place of honor at banquets and the best seats in the synagogues, and to be greeted with respect in the marketplaces, and to have people call them rabbi" (Matt. 23:5–7). Their self-absorption and excessive self-interest blind them to those in need, as happened with the priest and Levite in the parable of the good Samaritan (see Lk. 10:25–37).

- *A punctilious concern for the Church's liturgy, doctrine, and prestige*: Clergymen my age often joke that the only difference between a terrorist and the "liturgy police" (a derogatory term for people who take it upon themselves to obsess and monitor a clergyman's celebration of the sacraments to ensure everything is done according to the official rubrics of the Church) is that you can negotiate with a terrorist. I sometimes cringe when I hear the smug and holier-than-thou sentiments expressed on Catholic television and radio shows; I can't help wondering if the hosts and their listeners are simply pushing their own conservative theological agendas in defiance of the Church's social teachings and her engagement with contemporary culture.

- *A vanity about the ability to manage practical matters*: Modern-day Pelagians are the incarnations of Franklin Covey planners who pride themselves on their ability to organize their daily and weekly schedules while juggling recreation, family life, and career. This natural ability puffs them up and makes them look askance at people who seemingly bumble and muddle through the day.

- *An excessive concern with programs of self-help and personal fulfillment*: An Amazon search yields more than 70,000 self-help books in categories such as personal transformation, emotions, motivation, self-esteem, success, stress management, and happiness. This self-reliance on personal and spiritual growth is the very reason why Pelagianism is a heresy: it clearly shuts the door to the gift of divine grace working in one's life.

The Giftedness and Need for Grace

Holiness and transformation do not occur by our own self-imposed spiritual workout routine, no matter what it might entail: prayer techniques, ascetical practices, or retreat experiences. They only occur by grace and grace alone. "The Second Synod of Orange taught with firm authority that nothing human can demand, merit, or buy the gift of divine grace, and that all cooperation with it is a prior gift of that same grace" (53). At the very heart of our existence is the Creator's grace and giftedness.

Three times in this second chapter of the exhortation, the pontiff uses the word "progressive" (50, 56) when writing of the transformation that occurs through the gift of grace. Holiness doesn't happen in a flash. He notes how Pelagians fail to realize that human weaknesses are not instantaneously and completely healed by grace. He continues: "Grace, precisely because it builds on nature, does not make us superhuman all at once" (50). This is a clear affirmation of a popular saying, "I am a work in progress."

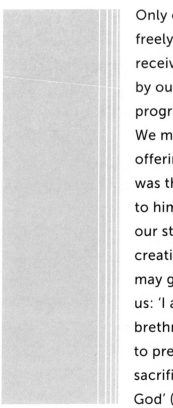

Only on the basis of God's gift, freely accepted and humbly received, can we cooperate by our own efforts in our progressive transformation. We must first belong to God, offering ourselves to him who was there first, and entrusting to him our abilities, our efforts, our struggle against evil and our creativity, so that his free gift may grow and develop within us: 'I appeal to you, therefore, brethren, by the mercies of God, to present your bodies as a living sacrifice, holy and acceptable to God' (*Rom* 12:1). (56)

This might be startling to some people. We should not be fixated on static perfection as a goal in our spiritual life. Unrealistic expectations and the mistaken belief in complete and superhuman transformation—sometimes expressed in questions such as, "Why do I still struggle with anger or sexual sins after all these years?", "How can I improve my prayer life?", or "How can I grow spiritually?"—suggest a subtle belief in Pelagianism. Though these questions point to meritorious desires, they also suggest that the spiritual journey is about manufactured perfection, not grace-given progress. With a smile on my face, I like to remind my directees: There is no such thing as a spiritual microwave oven you can jump into and come out, after thirty seconds, a saint. You have to jump into the crockpot called your life and slowly cook for an entire lifetime.

Spiritual Progress

Progress—for lack of a better word—in the spiritual life is not based on human effort but on "opening the door to grace" (35). That's why we need to grow in attentiveness to our subconscious attitudes and inadvertent behaviors that hijack, sabotage, or shut the door to the action of grace. Pondering questions such as "What is God asking of me in this situation?", "What attitude of mine is God challenging?", or "How might I respond more deeply to this invitation from God?" highlight and confirm the slow, progressive, and lifelong response to God's continual offer of grace.

Opening the door to grace with its accompanying spiritual growth is made possible by charity. Pope Francis quotes St. Paul, "'[I]f I do not have love, I am nothing' (*1 Cor* 13:2)" (56). In a beautiful sentence verging on mysticism, the pope writes: "[Jesus] gives us two faces, or better yet, one alone: the face of God reflected in so many other faces. For in every one of our brothers and sisters, especially the least, the most vulnerable, the defenseless and those in need, God's very image is found" (61). Love not only opens the door to grace but also the eyes to the vision of God.

I am reminded of the story about St. Vincent de Paul. The Daughters of Charity, the community of women he founded, wrote Vincent de Paul and asked him to resolve a dilemma: If they were praying in chapel and the doorbell rang, what should they do? Ignore the doorbell and keep praying or leave the chapel and answer the door? He responded, "Leave Christ in the chapel so you can meet him on your doorstep."

The road to holiness is not paved with hifalutin thoughts and finely honed theological theories. Nor is it found in esoteric experiences or by human excavation. It is a simple path of love and mercy that leads from the front door of a grace-inspired, open heart to the fringes of society, where the poor and marginalized shine with the face of God.

REFLECTION QUESTIONS

1. On the spiritual continuum, do you lean more toward the institutional Gnostic or the Spirit-led mystic? How do your thinking and beliefs control the action of God in your life, and how you assess the spiritual fitness of others?

2. Pope Francis reminds us in paragraph 42 that God is mysteriously present in the life of every single person, even someone riddled with vices and addictions. How can grace be present in the life of a notorious sinner, a mass murderer, or a convicted felon?

3. What attitudes and behaviors of yours hijack, sabotage, or shut the door of your heart to God's grace? How do you know when an attitude or behavior is doing that?

CHAPTER THREE

In the Light of the Master

I've spent the past few days asking friends and spiritual directees to define holiness. The variety of answers surprised me.

A Methodist minister said, "It's not just obeying God's commands and living a moral life, but holy people imitate Jesus." For him, holiness is connected to the teachings and actions of Jesus.

A fellow friar reminded me of Thomas Merton's definition: "Saints are people who, when they do their own will, are doing the will of God." This suggests a transformation of human desires. The will of the saint is united to the will of God.

One of my spiritual directees said that a holy person reflects God to the world, while another directee said, "Holiness is living your life based upon the reality that God is a loving Father."

My colleague Jessie finds Robert Mulholland's definition of spiritual formation quite helpful: "[T]he process of being conformed to the image of Christ for the sake of others."[1] As a process, holiness is not instantaneous, but evolves. The transformation is done *to* us, not by us. Our lives take on a Christlike quality. Holiness includes forgetting self and serving others.

The Auxiliary of the Archdiocese of Los Angeles, Bishop Robert Barron of www.WordonFire.org, sells a T-shirt on his website with his three paths to holiness: find the center (consciously acknowledge Christ as the ground and organizing center of your existence); realize you are a sinner (studying our lives in the light of Christ, we clearly see the distance between ourselves and the Lord); and recognize your life is not about you (Christ calls us to leave our ego-driven existence and take our place in his plan of love and redemption for the world). The first path puts Christ as number one in life. The second path is a radical blow to the ego. The third is the call to mission.

These definitions all highlight a few characteristics of Christian holiness: It's centered on Jesus Christ. It challenges and changes our ego-centered interests and instincts. It involves openness to others.

---

1. M. Robert Mulholland, Jr., *Invitation to a Journey: A Road Map for Spiritual Formation* (Downers Grove, IL: InterVarsity Press, 1993), 15.

The Beatitudes

So if anyone asks: "What must one do to be a good Christian?", the answer is clear. We have to do, each in our own way, what Jesus told us in the Sermon on the Mount. In the Beatitudes, we find a portrait of the Master, which we are called to reflect in our daily lives. (63)

In the third chapter of *Rejoice and Be Glad,* Pope Francis offers his understanding of practical holiness. It is rooted in the life and teaching of Jesus: "Jesus explained with great simplicity what it means to be holy when he gave us the Beatitudes (cf. *Mt* 5:3–12; *Lk* 6:20–23). The Beatitudes are like a Christian identity card" (63).

Acknowledging that the Greek word *makarios* can be translated as "happy" or "blessed," the pontiff says both words are synonyms for "holy." The Greek word "expresses the fact that those faithful to God and his word, by their self-giving, gain true happiness" (64).

The happiness and holiness attained by living the Beatitudes—and thus being true to one's real identity—are not easily received. They require an openness to the freeing power of the Holy Spirit and a countercultural way of thinking and living. In effect, a conversion. Pope Francis shows us the challenge as he walks us through each Beatitude. Let me comment on each of his reflections.

"Blessed are the poor in spirit, for theirs is the kingdom of heaven"

Where do you find your security? Sadly, many people find it in material possessions and wealth. The self-satisfaction that comes with wealth is dangerous because it consumes the heart, shutting its door and leaving "no room for God's word, for the love of our brothers and sisters, or for the enjoyment of the most important things in life. . . . That is why Jesus calls blessed those who are poor in spirit, those who have a poor heart, for there the Lord can enter with his perennial newness" (68). A simple, austere life opens the door to grace as we share in the life of the needy. This is how we "configure ourselves to Jesus who, though rich, 'made himself poor' (*2 Cor* 8:9)" (70).

Pope Francis's words jogged my memory. I didn't know why my spiritual director suggested an unusual exercise during my annual retreat. "Before you conclude your weeklong retreat, try this. Lie on the floor and pretend you have one hour to live. As you lie there, think about all your possessions—your books, your clothes, the money you squirreled away in your dresser drawer. Ask yourself, *How will this stuff help me make the transition to eternal life?*"

I never did the exercise. Just the thought of it made the point.

My spiritual director was clearly on the same wavelength as Pope Francis. Citing the parable of the rich fool who pulled down his barns and built bigger ones only to die that very day (see Lk. 12:16–21), the pope highlights the false security of possessions. The popular saying is true, "You can't take it with you when you die." The thought of death has a way of waking us up to life and realigning our priorities.

Is there another way we can monitor the influence that possessions have on us and, if necessary, realign our priorities? A second practical way is to pray over the monthly credit card bills. Look at how you spend your money. What do your charges say about your lifestyle? Are they mostly for necessities, or do they reveal a focus on the superfluous and extravagant? Is your spending stuffing your life with trinkets and treatments or is it suggesting a generous life of involvement with others? Your credit card bill speaks volumes about the open-door policy of your heart. "For where your treasure is, there your heart will be also" (Matt. 6:21).

Money and possessions are not our only refuge and security. We also become cozy, grow smug, and gloat over emotional investments in things like power, prestige, and popularity. Our Facebook postings and our tweets sometimes betray these emotional investments. Sadly, we are often unaware that like possessions, these bogus investments enslave us.

The pontiff reminds us, quoting the founder of the Jesuits, Ignatius of Loyola, that the path to holiness requires "'holy indifference' which brings us to a radiant interior freedom" (69). We are no longer attached, weighed down, or subconsciously controlled by our desires or obsessions for good health, riches, prestige, or a long life.

But how do we obtain that indifference and its accompanying interior freedom? It's a lifelong task requiring self-awareness and brutal self-honesty. I often invite my spiritual directees to reflect, ponder, and pray over their childhood and upbringing. So many of our attachments and obsessions are rooted in a childhood deficiency. As I once heard Trappist Thomas Keating put it, "What you lacked in your childhood or *think* you lacked in your childhood (perception shapes our reality), becomes your adult obsession." For example, adults raised in poverty or who think they never had enough, could easily develop an inordinate desire for money or possessions. Other times, adults feel they grew up in the shadows of a talented sibling; their emotional currency might be fame and prestige. Still others lacked attention or affection growing up and now have an emotional need to bargain in popularity or pleasure. Asking the questions, *What do I crave?*, *What do I think I need in order to be happy?*, as well as observing deep-seated desires and recurrent daydreams, can also be helpful in discovering and naming your personal currency.

Once we name our currency, we must realize it is counterfeit and has no real buying power. This is the wisdom of the first Beatitude. It categorically unmasks the worthlessness of a life invested in the passing values of this world and invites us to an alternative lifestyle—a life rich in poverty. "Blessed are the poor in spirit, for theirs is the kingdom of heaven. . . . Do not store up for yourselves treasures on earth, where moth and rust consume and where thieves break in and steal; but store up for yourselves treasures in heaven, where neither moth nor rust consumes and where thieves do not break in and steal" (Matt. 5:3, 6:19–20).

"Blessed are the meek, for they will inherit the earth"

Those who lacked attention and affirmation in childhood or were raised by controlling and overbearing parents often think pride and vanity will make them happy. This leads them to think they have the right to dominate others as they "constantly pigeonhole others on the basis of their ideas, their customs, and even their way of speaking or dressing" (71).

This air of superiority causes such people to expend a lot of emotional energy on "useless complaining." Citing Thérèse of Lisieux, *Gaudete et Exsultate* reminds us that "perfect charity consists in putting up with others' mistakes, and not being scandalized by their faults" (72).

The second Beatitude invites us to a life of humility, patience, and meekness. These three qualities—often lacking in the Church, as the pontiff notes—should govern not only how we correct others but also how we defend our beliefs and convictions. The countercultural paradox of the kingdom of God is unsettling: The arrogant and assertive are not the ultimate victors. The poor and meek, known in the Bible as the *anawim,* have their deepest desires fulfilled, see God's promises accomplished in their lives, and inherit the earth.

I sometimes see how my pride and vanity entice me to invest in impatience, annoyance, and irritation, and then to spend the dividends on those whom I consider unfortunate, incapable, or dull. I have to challenge myself to stop and stand in the other's shoes. I often remind myself of the advice given to me many years ago: "Most people are doing the best they can. If they *could* do better, they *would*. But right now, they *can't*, so they *don't*. You can't expect handicapped people to walk without a limp. And life being as it is, we all go around limping." Humility, patience, and meekness are fruits of compassion and understanding.

"Blessed are those who mourn, for they will be comforted"

I once met a Franciscan friar in Rome who was a gifted photographer. I was struck by one of the photographs taken in his native India. Its background was dominated by the Prestige Lakeside Habitat, a luxury-living community consisting of more than 3,500 high-rise apartments and 270 villas. In the foreground, a woman lay in front of a slum shanty with two of Mother Teresa's Missionaries of Charity, dressed in their distinctive white saris with blue-stripped borders, bent over and ministering to her. The contrast was jarring.

That photograph captured the pope's reflection on the third Beatitude. Some people have bought into the world's understanding of the good life: "entertainment, pleasure, diversion, and escape." Living in denial in their high-rise apartments, these people expend much emotional energy "fleeing from situations of sufferings in the belief that reality can be concealed" (75).

Then there are the people below, like Mother Teresa's missionaries, who face reality head on. They find true happiness by embracing the sufferings of others and engaging their painful circumstances. Pope Francis notes: "They sense that the other is flesh of our flesh, and are not afraid to draw near, even to touch their wounds" (76). Two opposing worlds meet and unite. Suffering meets solace in the stance of the saints.

To mourn with others is the essence of compassion. The Latin etymological roots of "compassion" are *cum* ("with") and *passio* ("suffer"). To "suffer with" others is a stunning reflection of the mission of Jesus, who entered our world of struggles and temptations. Compassion never destroys; it stretches the size of the heart and makes the distance between you and me vanish. In doing that, it makes us more human—and Christlike.

"Blessed are those who hunger and thirst for righteousness, for they will be filled"

It's a dog-eat-dog world with business-driven values. Those values are "marred by petty interests and manipulated in various ways." Corruption and tit-for-tat partisan politics often prey on city, state, and national governments. Consequently, some people are left behind while "others divvy up the good things of this life," and well-intentioned people, grown discouraged, "opt to follow in the train of the winners" (78).

Some people have an instinct for the kingdom's justice and righteousness. This longing is satisfied not only when they are just in their own decision-making process but also when they pursue justice for the poor and weak. Not wanting to let the challenge of justice be watered down and soft-pedaled by its synonym— "faithfulness to God's will in every aspect of our life"—Pope Francis, quoting Isaiah, states: "If we give the word too general a meaning, we forget that it is shown especially in justice towards those who are most vulnerable: 'Seek justice, correct oppression; defend the fatherless, plead for the widow (*Is* 1:17)'" (79).

More so than any other Beatitude, especially in our time with the crises of the refugees in Europe and the undocumented immigrants in the United States, this is challenging—and, as I have learned from experience, controversial in its implications.

A Roman Catholic permanent deacon began a spiritual direction session by telling me about his thirty-fifth wedding anniversary.

"Congratulations," I said. "What a wonderful witness both of you give to me and to your family and friends. How did you celebrate?"

"You won't believe it, Father, but I managed to get reservations at Oriole. You know, it was rated two stars by Michelin and only seats twenty-eight people a night."

"Wow! That must have cost you a small fortune."

"It did! Without the tip, it came to over $650," smacking his lips with relish and satisfaction.

I paused for a moment and hesitated to say what was on my mind. But in the end, I did.

"Deacon Bill, you are an ordained deacon in the Church and have the example of Pope Francis as a guide. Help me to understand how you could justify spending so much money on one meal, especially when there are so many poor people in the world."

His body jerked and his eyes flashed at me. He turned beet red. And suddenly, he silently stood up and walked out of my office. I never saw him again.

As a spiritual director and companion myself, I have found the pope's understanding of justice one of the most difficult topics to broach in spiritual direction. Directees, often blinded by their sense of entitlement and the agenda of their particular political party, fidget in their seats and sometimes become defensive. They have no problem talking about their struggles in prayer and the challenges with fasting and other acts of mortification. But when a spiritual director raises the issues of almsgiving, our relationship to the poor, and our vocation to be the voice for the voiceless, the conversation can become difficult—or, as it did with Deacon Bill, come to a complete halt.

Social justice is a topic that can never be over-emphasized. This is why many of us consider our spiritual companion Pope Francis a gift to the Church—while others consider him their nemesis. Every day he challenges us and models for us how to open the door of the heart to the poor, the migrant, the immigrant, and the forgotten of society. His critics are many, and that makes me wonder if they have simply opted "to follow in the train of the winners" (78).

"Blessed are the merciful, for they will receive mercy"

Rejoice and Be Glad reminds us that mercy is one coin with two sides. One side is giving, helping, and serving others. The other side is forgiveness and understanding. Based on the Golden Rule, mercy is almsgiving we continually offer, especially when we disagree and take exception to other people's moral judgments and decisions.

Our attempts to give and forgive lamely reflect God's perfection, "which gives and forgives superabundantly" (81). Luke records Jesus's command: "Be merciful, even as your Father is merciful. Judge not, and you will not be judged; condemn not, and you will not be condemned; forgive, and you will be forgiven; give, and it will be given to you. The measure you give will be the measure you get back" (Lk. 6:36–38). It's a thought worth pondering daily: we ourselves determine the yardstick of divine grace and forgiveness used upon us—and it is the same size we use upon others.

Even knowing that, we still too easily, too often sit in judgment on the decisions of others. We question another's decision about their spouse, their lifestyle, or their business and respond with the cold shoulder, the chilling silence, the grimace and raised eyebrow, or a feigned deafness to their request.

How do we rid ourselves of this smug, judgmental attitude? How can we nurture the apostolic exhortation's understanding of mercy as service and forgiveness? One typical way is to imitate what Jesus did in the Incarnation: put ourselves in the other's shoes, ponder their situation, and pray for the light of the Spirit. Only the most hardhearted can stand in judgment when wearing the other's shoes. Mercy and compassion are gifts the saints give others— and God returns the favor.

"Blessed are the pure of heart, for they will see God"

According to the Bible, the heart is the seat of "our real intentions, the things we truly seek and desire" (83). And what is the one intention that we should truly seek and desire? Page after page of *Gaudete et Exsultate* reminds us: "a commitment to our brothers and sisters that comes from the heart" (85). Pope Francis sums up this Beatitude when he writes, "A heart that loves God and neighbor (cf. *Mt* 22:36–40), genuinely and not merely in words, is a pure heart; it can see God" (86).

Opening the door of the heart to this grace includes an examination of those attitudes and actions that jeopardize our love for God and others. This is the practical holiness envisioned by the pontiff. Because we are masters of self-deception who can rationalize or justify any belief or action, this examination can be aided by a second pair of ears—and a well-trained tongue. Asking open-ended, non-judgmental questions, an experienced spiritual director or companion can help us discover biases and prejudices that not only sabotage our relationships with God and others, but also hinder us from seeing the divine image and likeness in our neighbors. Purity of heart is a grace, a goal, and a discipline.

It's important to remember that we are born pure of heart. We *learn* to be biased and prejudiced because of our nationality, race, gender, color, creed, upbringing, social conditioning, political beliefs, life experience, and family status, to name just a few factors. Being born again (see John 3:3), becoming like a child (see Matt. 18:3), and unlearning our skewed prejudgments are challenging, but not impossible, spiritual disciplines.

As spiritual disciplines, they begin with awareness: identify your blind spots. If you're interested in discovering your hidden biases favoring or disfavoring certain groups and naming your possible prejudices against people of certain races, religions, or sexual identities, you might want to visit Harvard University's "Project Implicit" at https://implicit.harvard.edu/implicit/takeatest.html. You'll find a number of free, ten-minute Implicit Association Tests that might help you discover where bias, chauvinism, bigotry, sexism, or discrimination is hindering your vision of God enfleshed in other people.

Purifying the mind and softening the heart continue with the process of deliberately challenging and changing your thinking—ingrained thoughts, though acknowledged, don't simply dissipate or go up in smoke on their own. Compassion again can play a role: go online and learn about this particular group's history, its struggles, and its challenges. Prayerfully put yourself in the group's shoes and see how it feels to be a member.

If possible, befriend a member of the group. You might be surprised to discover that beyond the caustic and vitriolic label you slapped on the member stands a person with flesh and blood, a name, a history, and struggles similar to your own.

Consider where your biases and prejudices find support. Distance yourself from relatives and friends who have promoted your former beliefs based on their ignorance, hatred, or fear—accept the fact that you might end up sacrificing a friend or two in the process. Be attentive and choose not to listen to one-sided television and radio personalities who spew fearful, hateful rhetoric. Refuse to support politicians whose diatribes are based on their own megalomania, self-interests, and hidden agendas.

As your vision improves and your heart is purified, you might consider actively supporting organizations that fight prejudice and discrimination—or even joining them. Organizations like the American Civil Liberties Union, the Southern Poverty Law Center, and the National Association for the Advancement of Colored People are three that immediately come to mind.

Purity of heart is a graced discipline. As we deliberately choose to open the door of our hearts and roll out the welcome mat to all people, we discover, perhaps for the first time, "the face of God reflected in so many other faces" (61).

"Blessed are the peacemakers, for they will be called children of God"

The pontiff's reflections on this Beatitude surprise me. Rather than focus on global politics and the reality of wars between nations, he pinpoints the source of those conflicts: the individual. He mentions those negative people who spread gossip and snicker at its harm. In a footnote, he refers to detraction (revealing a person's real faults to a third person, thereby lessening the reputation of that person) and calumny (making false and defamatory statements in order to damage a person's reputation) as "acts of terrorism" (footnote 73). In footnote 74, he notes how an emotionally charged interpretation is sometimes passed on as fact; this misconstrues the reality of the situation, thus disrespecting both the facts themselves and the person involved.

To "make" Gospel peace means excluding no one, including "those who are a bit odd, troublesome or difficult, demanding, different, beaten down by life or simply uninterested." Evangelical peace is not consensus, something the minority can reluctantly live with, or a denial of conflict. It requires a finesse that faces the conflict, resolves it, and then incorporates it into a new process. That happens through honest, one-on-one dialogue, listening, and compassionate understanding—in other words, opening the door of one's heart. Pope Francis highlights the challenge of true peacemaking: "We need to be artisans of peace, for building peace is a craft that demands serenity, creativity, sensitivity and skill" (89).

Many people look to the Franciscans as peacemaking experts. They might know the famous story of Saint Francis going to Damietta, Egypt, in 1219 to negotiate peace between the Christian Crusaders and the Muslim sultan. We do not know what the saint and the sultan talked about while Francis was in the sultan's camp, but we do know the conversation's effect on each: In the revised Rule of 1221, Francis wrote that the friars who want to go among the Muslims should not quarrel with them or cause disputes, "but be subject to every human creature for God's sake

(1 Pet. 2:13) and confess that they are Christians." After flooding the Christian camp with the waters of the Nile, the sultan chose not to kill the incapacitated Christians but to send them daily bread for survival. Clearly, Saint Francis of Assisi and Sultan Malik al-Kamil had opened the doors of their hearts to one another.

Francis of Assisi is wrongly credited as the author of the Peace Prayer that bears his name. Though the prayer's association with the saint dates back only to the beginning of the twentieth century, the prayer offers some important strategies for peacemaking that the saint and sultan used with each other: sowing love, pardon, hope and seeking to console, understand, and love. Such individual, other-centered actions are a sure way to lay a foundation for practical holiness and global peace.

"Blessed are those who are persecuted for righteousness' sake, for theirs is the kingdom of heaven"

This final Beatitude reminds us of the fundamental instrument of our holiness: "[T]he cross remains the source of our growth and sanctification" (92). If we live a countercultural lifestyle that struggles for justice and is committed to God and others, we will become a "nuisance" (90) to society. And society's response? In the most extreme case, martyrdom. But for most of us, the response will be a subtler persecution as people slander us, lie about us, denigrate our faith, and make us look ridiculous. Jesus said we are blessed when people "utter all kinds of evil against us falsely on my account" (Matt. 5:11).

The obsession with our reputations and what people think of us drive us to fly below the radar screen, bury our heads, occasionally look over our shoulders, and overthink before standing up for Gospel values. In order to keep a superficial peace and avoid criticism, we tend to keep our mouths shut, saying nothing about overcharging for billable hours, unjustly firing a coworker, blatantly favoring or belittling a child, or ignoring the elephant in the room. "Play nice" was my grandmother's advice. That can easily translate into an "obscure mediocrity" (90) where we temporarily save our life only to lose it for eternity.

"You did it to me."

Those who really wish to give glory to God by their lives, who truly long to grow in holiness, are called to be single-minded and tenacious in their practice of the works of mercy. (107)

The third chapter of *Rejoice and Be Glad* includes what the pontiff considers to be the great criterion for our judgment: "'I was hungry and you gave me food, I was thirsty and you gave me drink, I was a stranger and you welcomed me, I was naked and you clothed me, I was sick and you took care of me, I was in prison and you visited me' (Mt 25:35–36)" (95). Holiness is not about "swooning in mystic rapture" but recognizing "in the poor and the suffering . . . the very heart of Christ, his deepest feelings and choices" (96). Pope Francis asks that the uncompromising demands of Jesus be accepted in a literal way and continues, "In other words, without any 'ifs or buts' that could lessen their force. Our Lord made it very clear that holiness cannot be understood or lived apart from these demands, for mercy is 'the beating heart of the Gospel'" (97).

I have heard many a priest preach about the need to see Christ in the poor and marginalized of society. This seems to be a standard bullet point of any homily about the parable of the Judgment of the Nations from the twenty-fifth chapter of Matthew. But I have never heard anyone tell me *how* to see Christ in them. Pope Francis suggests it's about my attitude and having a spiritual vision. Rather than seeing a poor person as an annoyance or a social problem that politicians need to address, as a Christian I am being asked to have a very different, countercultural perspective: responding with faith and charity, I see in the marginalized person "a human being with a dignity identical to my own, a creature infinitely loved by the Father, an image of God, a brother or sister redeemed by Jesus Christ" (98). This is practical holiness.

I instantly thought of Mother Teresa of Calcutta's "five-finger gospel." A British reporter was shadowing Mother Teresa as she brought dying people to her home and fed them. The reporter asked, "Mother, what are you thinking as you care for this dying man?" Mother Teresa looked up, held up her right hand, and as she individually bent each of her five fingers, very methodically responded, "You. Did. It. To. Me."

Faith and Action Combined

The pope mentions two errors that arise when we separate our faith from the merciful action it requires. One is to so overemphasize the Gospel demands for mercy that they are no longer informed by our relationship with God and openness to divine grace. Suddenly, Christianity is reduced to philanthropy. Or, in the pontiff's words, Christianity "becomes a sort of NGO stripped of the luminous mysticism" (100) that fueled the lives of the saintly lovers of the poor like Francis of Assisi, Vincent de Paul, and Mother Teresa of Calcutta. Prayer and love for God propelled these people to an effective engagement and passionate love for others.

The other error is to so overemphasize the spiritual life that our merciful engagement with others is seen as "superficial, worldly, secular, materialist, communist or populist" (101). Or, we canonize one ethical issue like defense of the innocent unborn, for example, while giving lesser importance to the lives of the poor, those already born, the destitute, the vulnerable infirm, and the elderly. To be pro-life is to adopt the Seamless Garment doctrine of the late Cardinal Bernardine of Chicago and support life in all its forms from conception to natural death—including the poor, the prisoner, and the undocumented.

The pope, quoting the Rule of Saint Benedict, expressly references migrants and strangers among those who should be welcomed "like Christ" (102). Fending off his critics, he notes, "This is not a notion invented by some Pope, or a momentary fad" (103); rather, it is rooted in the wisdom of the Old Testament, especially the prophet Isaiah.

Prayer's Purpose

Some of us on occasion question the quality of our Sunday worship: are our songs and prayers pleasing to God? Others are dissatisfied with their personal, private prayer: how can they grow it and deepen it? Pope Francis is unrelenting in judging the quality of our worship of God and personal prayer: "Our worship becomes pleasing to God when we devote ourselves to living generously, and allow God's gift, granted in prayer, to be shown in our concern for our brothers and sisters. Similarly, the best way to discern if our prayer is authentic is to judge to what extent our life is being transformed in the light of mercy" (104–105).

The implications of practical holiness can be unsettling. Some people might think the addition of more "smells and bells" to the liturgy coupled with uplifting songs is more pleasing to God or prayer in total silence with no distractions is more reverent. The pope as a spiritual companion points my attention neither to the heavens nor to my head; rather, he calls my attention to a neighbor in need. Jesus himself says a tree is known by its fruit (see Lk. 6:43–44). Am I growing in love, mercy, and forgiveness? Am I growing in sensitivity to the poor and marginalized? The pontiff writes, "Those who really wish to give glory to God by their lives, who truly long to grow in holiness, are called to be single-minded and tenacious in their practice of the works of mercy" (107).

Catholic tradition offers us seven spiritual works of mercy and seven corporal works of mercy. The spiritual works of mercy are these: instruct the ignorant, counsel the doubtful, admonish sinners, forgive offenses, comfort the afflicted, bear wrongs patiently, and pray for the living and the dead. The seven corporal works of mercy are these: feed the hungry, give drink to the thirsty, shelter the homeless, clothe the naked, visit the sick, visit the imprisoned, and bury the dead.

These spiritual and corporal works of mercy call us to be attentive to others. They show the practical consequences of a life of love, a life of practical holiness. Periodically review these works of mercy and ask yourself how God might be calling them forth. This would indicate not only your ability to listen to the Spirit in prayer but also the openness of your heart to grace. If none of these works of mercy are apparent in your life, you might want to revisit the quality and practice of your prayer life. Perhaps you look upon your prayer and other spiritual practices more as tasks to be completed and less as the fuel to move beyond the ego.

A Final Challenge

The third chapter of *Gaudete et Exsultate* concludes with a warning about hedonism and consumerism, signs of the bottomless pit of the ego with its appetite for gratification. Pope Francis again calls us to "a certain simplicity of life, resisting the feverish demands of a consumer society, which leave us impoverished and unsatisfied, anxious to have it all now" (108).

The pope also mentions our obsession with the digital age and its superficial information, instant communication, and virtual reality. These keep us fixated on the ego and our personal pleasure. This fixation dulls our senses and makes us insensitive and indifferent "to the suffering flesh of our brothers and sisters" (108).

Pope Francis reminds us that "Christianity is meant above all to be put into practice" (109). He has shown us in this central chapter of the apostolic exhortation just how practical and challenging holiness is. And yet, for twenty-one centuries, its expression has remained the same: love of God is measured in love of neighbor.

REFLECTION QUESTIONS

1. What areas of your life do the Beatitudes challenge? What needs to change in your life in order to live the Beatitudes fully?

2. Prayerfully read and reflect upon Matthew 25:31–46. In what ways are you ranked among the sheep? In what ways are you ranked among the goats?

3. How much time and energy do you spend on social media? How do you know when this is a convenient distraction or a sinful form of egotistical self-indulgence? How many of your tweets and Facebook postings are about you and your accomplishments?

CHAPTER FOUR

Signs of Holiness in Today's World

H ow do I know if I am growing in holiness?" "What does spiritual progress look like?" "How do you know someone is a saint?" These questions are occasionally asked during spiritual direction sessions.

I skirt these questions when I suspect a directee is trying to measure how well he or she might stack up to the saints. To be concerned about answers to such questions keeps the spotlight on oneself and could devolve into spiritual pride—"Look at me! I'm making progress!"—or discouragement—"I'll never overcome this sin."

My response is always the same. "Holiness is extraordinarily personal. There's no 'one-size-fits-all' checklist." I then encourage the person to continue not only being attentive to God's grace to die to the ego but also being responsive to God's call to move toward a neighbor.

However, when I am presenting one of my workshops on the spiritual life and such questions are asked, I do, in fact, attempt an answer. I point to the fifth chapter of Paul's Letter to the Galatians where the Apostle to the Gentiles lists the nine fruit of the Holy Spirit. Those nine fruit are a good yardstick for the action of the Spirit and what it perennially means to live like Christ, to be a saint.

The Nine Fruit of the Spirit

LOVE moves me beyond the hurts and grudges that hinder me from acknowledging others. It opens my heart unreservedly so I can be accepting and attentive to the needs of any person, no matter who he is or how she might live. Not always a feeling, love is the commitment that fashions me to live the Golden Rule without thought or hesitation; it challenges me to will the good of the other.

JOY deepens my experience of life as I stand in wonder and awe of the universe, the solar system, planet Earth, the trees and the apples they bear, my spouse, and this daffodil at my feet—all gifts given by the Creator for my enjoyment and use. "All this and heaven too!" It is an exuberance shaped by the firmly grounded faith and hope in Christ's resurrection. It moves me beyond worries and anxieties.

The Spirit's PEACE blocks saints from passively supporting or actively promoting the violence that arises from apathy, prejudice, sexism, and discrimination. It impels them, as they stand up and speak out for justice on behalf of the voiceless and marginalized, to urge dialogue, understanding, and compassion.

PATIENCE replaces the knee-jerk reaction of anger. The patient person no longer fights against the things that cannot be changed and no longer refuses to accept the inconveniences of daily life. This fruit encourages surrender and acceptance. It instills the desire and willingness to persevere, persist, and promote one's relationship with God, others, and the self.

Some people, living outside the aches, wants, demands, and desires of their skin, sparkle with KINDNESS. They are compassionate, helpful, generous, and caring. "It's my pleasure. I'm happy to help you"—and they mean it!

GENEROUS people are never stingy or selfish. Nor are they self-absorbed, self-obsessed, or self-seeking. They have a knack for not only seeing the poor on the street but also responding to them. "It's just a five-dollar bill," they say. They give—and receive in abundance.

FAITHFULNESS has two sides. One is the profound loyalty and dedication to public commitments like promises and vows made to spouses, relatives, communities, friends, and coworkers. The other side is living a life "full of faith" in God's love, providence, and forgiveness.

As I grow in GENTLENESS, I no longer bang my fist on the table, raise my voice, pull strings behind the scene, or manipulate situations to make sure I get my way and remain in control. I am never blunt, brash, brazen, or brusque. Spiritual gentleness breeds godly graciousness.

To live like Christ is to be interiorly free from the hedonistic demands and fleeting impulses of the ego. This is the Spirit's SELF-CONTROL. It teaches me to ignore the circus barker who tempts and lures, to simply walk past the tent leading to temptation and sin. I am no longer a prisoner of my self-centeredness or a slave to my passions.

Saints are not people who have blossomed with each and every fruit of the Holy Spirit. They typically live one in an outstanding and heroic way. Think of Julia Greeley and her generosity, Stanley Rother and his faithfulness, Vincent de Paul and his kindness, Mother Teresa of Calcutta and her love, and Philip Neri and his joy. They struggled, were weak, and had foibles, yet shone because they perennially bore just one spiritual fruit in a marvelous manner.

Great Expressions of Love

In chapter four of *Rejoice and Be Glad*, Pope Francis offers his own answer to the question, "How do you know someone is a saint?" He does not want to explain certain spiritual practices that are helpful to spiritual growth, but instead wants to speak "only of certain aspects of the call to holiness that I hope will prove especially meaningful" (110).

In an anxious world filled with negativity, consumerism, individualism, and "ersatz spirituality—having nothing to do with God" (111), the pontiff offers five great expressions of love for God and neighbor that he considers particularly important. Clearly not spiritual practices per se and certainly not exclusive, these are attitudes or "great signs" (112) we need to grow as we open the door of our hearts to grace and walk our unique and individual path to holiness.

Grounded in God

The inner strength of the saint comes from a "solid grounding in the God who loves and sustains us" (112). After stating this first characteristic, the pontiff quotes Scripture liberally and offers broad reflections on its three effects: perseverance, patience, and meekness.

This grounding builds up perseverance amid the challenges of daily living. In a fast-paced and aggressive world, this perseverance is expressed through patience and constancy in doing good. Highlighting again how love of God and neighbor are two sides of the same coin and playing on a Greek word, Pope Francis writes: "It is a sign of the fidelity born of love, for those who put their faith in God (*pistis*) can also be faithful to others (*pistos*)" (112). A saint never ceases to accompany those in need and always stands with them, no matter how unsatisfying and difficult their situations may be.

Being grounded in God fosters meekness, the virtue that short-circuits attitudinal, verbal, and physical violence. It begins with a nonviolent approach to life that, despite its weak appearance, is a sign of true strength.

The strength of meekness lies in its ability not only to recognize aggressive and selfish inclinations but also to eliminate them before they take root. This includes not getting caught up in the verbal violence sometimes promoted on the Web and in digital communication such as posting inflammatory, extraneous, or off-topic messages to provoke readers, a practice called trolling; insulting others with profanity or teaming up with others to hurt someone, a practice called flaming. It also requires holding our tongue before the faults of others. Meek people don't have the emotional need to verbally demean or mistreat others.

We all know the satisfaction that comes with verbal abuse, don't we? We're sometimes surprised by what causes our outburst. We're under a lot of tension and stress. Perhaps we feel pressured to meet an imminent deadline. Maybe we're burdened with worries as we await the results of a medical test. A teenager might be getting underneath our skin and pushing all our buttons. Suddenly, a spouse or friend or even a stranger grimaces, sneers, or scowls— and we explode in anger, spewing regretful words like a pressure cooker opened too quickly.

Simple awareness can be helpful here. So much of our attitudinal, verbal, or physical violence is born of a knee-jerk reaction to a situation when we aren't in touch with our thoughts and feelings. Briefly pausing and asking three simple questions—*What am I thinking? What am I feeling? What would Jesus do?*—can root us in the present moment and make us conscious of an appropriate response, rather than an instinctual reaction. The pope points our attention to a well-known fact when he notes, "[P]eople look to compensate for their own discomfort by lashing out at others" (115). Simply being aware of any personal discomfort is one way to hijack a reaction that we might later regret.

Another form of violence, subtler in approach, acts like a wolf in sheep's clothing: to look down on others and lord it over them by trying to teach them lessons. Footnote 95 of Pope Francis's *Rejoice and Be Glad* mentions "some forms of bullying that, while seeming delicate or respectful and even quite spiritual, cause great damage to others' self-esteem." The parent or in-law, for example, who is always mildly suggesting how to raise a grandchild or overtly correcting parenting techniques, is a perpetrator of this kind of subtle violence. Every word of correction, sometimes draped in spiritual advice—"This will be good for your spiritual growth"—erodes the other's confidence and self-worth. I'm sure we have all met children, or even adults, who have had the glint in their eyes extinguished because of overbearing parents or controlling spouses. The pontiff quotes John of the Cross who advised his spiritual directees to always prefer to be taught by all rather than to desire teaching even the least of all.

More than a pope or pastor, Pope Francis reveals himself to be an insightful and practical spiritual companion as he indicates the door leading to meekness: "Humility can only take root in the heart through humiliations. Without them, there is no humility or holiness. If you are unable to suffer and offer up a few humiliations, you are not humble and you are not on the path to holiness. . . . Humiliation makes you resemble Jesus; it is an unavoidable aspect of the imitation of Christ" (118). While martyrdom is the classic example of humiliation, Pope Francis notes the humiliations that come from holding one's tongue, praising others rather than boasting, choosing to do the less favorite or popular tasks, and the willingness to bear injustice.

However, don't get the impression that humility is all about docility, passivity, or inaction. The pope is wise enough to know otherwise: "At times, precisely because someone is free of selfishness, he or she can dare to disagree gently, to demand justice or to defend the weak before the powerful, even if it may harm his or her reputation" (119). Meekness is ultimately being "freed from the aggressiveness born of overweening egotism" (121).

How can we root ourselves in this solid grounding in God with its three spiritual effects that *Gaudete et Exultate* promotes as the first sign of holiness? One practical way would be to consider the "methodless method" of prayer taught by a seventeenth-century sandal maker, wine buyer, and cook, Carmelite Brother Lawrence of the Resurrection.

Brother Lawrence neither taught a method or technique nor had a gimmick for prayer. He simply talked about the importance of speaking and doing everything with the awareness that God is present. A practical way of promoting this realization is thinking of ourselves as fish in a fishbowl and that fishbowl is God. Or turn it into a technique: use Paul's statement at the Areopagus, "For 'In him we live and move and have our being'" (Acts 17:28) as a prayer phrase that is slowly repeated and coordinated with your breathing. Pope Francis had written earlier in the apostolic exhortation, "So often we say that God dwells in us, but it is better to say that we dwell in him, that he enables us to dwell in his light and love" (51). Think of God's love as the air you breathe and God's light as the ability to see your feet even at night. Just sit with this awareness uppermost in your mind and breathe. Just breathe. This practice of the divine presence builds confidence in God's abiding providence and becomes a firm grounding for daily living.

Added to that awareness of being in God are an honest self-assessment and spiritual direction. Both will deepen the awareness and knowledge of your reactive thoughts and feelings, enlightening you to the innumerable ways the neurotic and combative ego resists and repels humiliations. Forewarned is forearmed—and you can sabotage the ego's reaction by intentionally surrendering to and accepting humiliation. That acceptance combined with the awareness of God's abiding presence will encourage you to pray and live the crucified Jesus's prayer of surrender, "Father, into your hands I commend my spirit" (Luke 23:46). It's a paradox in the lives of the saints: letting go and free-falling show the depth of their grounding in God.

Joy

I recommend praying the prayer attributed to Saint Thomas More: "Grant me, O Lord, good digestion, and also something to digest. Grant me a healthy body, and the necessary good humor to maintain it. Grant me a simple soul that knows to treasure all that is good and that doesn't frighten easily at the sight of evil, but rather finds the means to put things back in their place. Give me a soul that knows not boredom, grumbling, sighs and laments, nor excess of stress, because of that obstructing thing called 'I'. Grant me, O Lord, a sense of good humor. Allow me the grace to be able to take a joke and to discover in life a bit of joy, and to be able to share it with others." (footnote 101)

In seven short paragraphs with more than twenty scriptural citations, Pope Francis explores the second sign of contemporary holiness. "Far from being timid, morose, acerbic or melancholy, or putting on a dreary face, the saints are joyful and full of good humor. Though completely realistic, they radiate a positive and hopeful spirit" (122). This joy is based on the certainty that God infinitely loves them and brings with it "deep security, serene hope and a spiritual fulfillment that the world cannot understand or appreciate" (125). Radically different from the passing pleasures that our individualistic and consumer society lamely offers, saintly joy is countercultural because it looks beyond the ego, to giving rather than receiving, to rejoicing in the good of others.

"Sadness," according to the pontiff, "can be a sign of ingratitude" (126). One of my spiritual directees, Carlita, would now agree. She's a single mother of twins and works hard to make ends meet. During our first spiritual direction session, she seemed downcast and forlorn and very much caught up in her personal struggles. At the conclusion of our session, I did something that I normally don't do. I gave her some homework.

"Before our next visit, spend some time every day making a list of all the things for which you are grateful. It can be something small like an email from a friend or something big like having the money to pay the bills. Also think of the most difficult challenges from your past. How did you manage? How did you jump over the hurdles?"

I was surprised when Carlita returned for our second session with a small spiral notebook with a number of pages full. *Here's a serious student*, I thought. I was amazed at her change in attitude.

"This was an incredible exercise," she said. "Never in my wildest dreams did I consider myself blessed by God. But you know what? God has taken care of me even when I didn't know it. When the father of my twins disappeared, God opened doors for me to get a basic education at the local community college. And that led me to getting a job as a dental assistant. And just the other day, when I was thinking how hard life is, I got a surprise phone call from a friend who always has a kind word and who knows how to lighten my mood. This homework taught me that God is as tightly bound up in my life as the threads on my blouse."

Just this simple exercise of intentionally reflecting upon her life changed Carlita's attitude—and it can change ours as well. It stirs the embers, sparking a confidence and security to endure the most trying of times. Acknowledging God as the source of everything good in our lives flares into the prayer of gratitude and makes us glow with joy.

Meister Eckhart is often quoted as saying, "If the only prayer you ever pray is 'Thank you, Lord', that is enough." As sadness shows ingratitude, joy shines and shimmers with gratitude.

Beyond Your Comfort Zone

There's a third sign of contemporary holiness. To obtain it, we must overcome an obstacle very different from sadness. It's a heavier, clunkier, and more unwieldly stumbling block that establishes its own egocentric center of gravity, holding us tightly, and, as I've seen, sometimes starting when we are in our twenties. If we are not consciously aware of it, we can become entrenched in its paralyzing fear and excessive caution.

We have all heard—and said—the time-honored excuses for sitting on the fence and becoming complacent: "If it ain't broke, don't fix it." "There's nothing I can do about it." "We've always done it this way." "Don't go upsetting the applecart." We need "to stop trying to make our Christian life a museum of memories" (139), as Pope Francis so memorably puts it.

Comparing us to the prophet Jonah who initially refused God's summons to preach repentance to the people of Nineveh and instead went to Joppa and sailed for Tarshish, the apostolic exhortation states, "[W]e are constantly tempted to flee to a safe haven" (134). *Rejoice and Be*

Glad highlights ten of those safe havens, all pointing to just how "seductive" (137) complacency is:

- *Individualism*: This is the obsession endemic to American culture. Life is about me and my concerns. I call the shots. I don't need anyone since I am independent and self-reliant.
- *Spiritualism*: This is self-absorption with the spiritual life to the detriment of physical reality. Attempting to live like an angel, the person focuses so much on growth in the spiritual life with prayer and penitential practices, that one walks past the poor on the street and is blind to the marginalized of society. This person lives from the mistaken notion that the spiritual life is more about the spirit and less about life.
- *Living in a little world*: Some people, deliberately choosing to be oblivious to what is happening in the wider world, retreat to their hermitage. Like an ostrich, they bury their heads in the sand.
- *Addiction*: When we become smug about an unhealthy or bad habit, it snatches control of our lives. We chain-smoke, pour the third glass of Scotch, watch Home Shopping Network and max out on the credit card. Physically stuck and psychologically compelled to repeat what we know is detrimental, we lose our freedom and ability to change, to grow, to improve.

- *Intransigence*: This is the deliberate refusal to change and the willful resistance to improve. With heels dug in, we bow to the status quo.
- *The rejection of new ideas and approaches*: Closed to creativity and fearing the unknown, we reject any new way of thinking or doing something.
- *Dogmatism*: This is the blind insistence that certain principles are incontrovertibly true and non-negotiable. Case closed. Period.
- *Nostalgia*: Some people have a sentimental longing and wistful affection for the past. "Oh, for the good old days!" They canonize their memories and complain about the deficiency of the present.
- *Pessimism*: The party pooper, the prophet of doom, the sourpuss, and the killjoy lack confidence and hope in the future. Their eyeglasses are smudged with disappointment, failure, pain, and the worst-case scenario.
- *Hiding behind rules and regulations*: Sticklers give every rule and regulation the same weight of importance, insisting each be literally obeyed. They insist that paperwork, policy, and procedures are more important than people with their problems.

These safe havens sometimes overlap and all have the same purpose in mind: to resist "leaving behind a familiar and easy way of doing things" (134).

Enter saintly missionaries. They make us feel uncomfortable because they challenge our complacency and mediocrity. They are not content to remain close to the shore but dare to put out into the deep, where the complacent can't even imagine going, and journeying to the fringes where Jesus resides "in the hearts of our brothers and sisters, in their wounded flesh, in their troubles and in their profound desolation" (135).

These people possess *parrhesia*. Pope Francis chooses to use the Greek word because, like a diamond, it has many facets including "boldness, enthusiasm, the freedom to speak out, apostolic fervor," all pointing to "the freedom of a life open to God and to others" (129). The boldness and apostolic courage of this third sign, the pope notes, catapulted Jesus not only to go out and preach but also to send the apostles to heal and liberate others. Pope Francis invites us to pray for *parrhesia* so that "the Church will not stand still, but constantly welcome the Lord's surprises" (139).

Roman Catholicism has a rich tradition of missionaries whose *parrhesia* propelled them to take the Gospel not only to their own people but also to far and exotic places. I think of the twentieth-century Italian Franciscan Gabriele

Allegra, who was stationed in Hong Kong and translated the entire Bible into Chinese; the twentieth-century Ursuline Dorothy Kazel, who was beaten, raped, and murdered in El Salvador; the sixteenth-century Portuguese missionary Francisco Álvares, sent to Ethiopia; the late nineteenth-century German-born American Marianne Cope, who ministered to the lepers of Molokai; the nineteenth-century French missionary François Bourgade, who was one of the first missionaries to Muslim North Africa; the twentieth-century Japanese Theresia Unno, who helped build churches and houses in the Philippines; the sixteenth-century Jesuit Francis Xavier, missionary to India and China; and the nineteenth-century Chinese martyr Lucy Yi Zhenmei. Such saintly people remind us that the third sign of contemporary holiness, *parrhesia*, is used for the service of mission.

Though not all of us are called or in a position to leave our country for a foreign land to proclaim the Gospel with *parrhesia*, nevertheless, we are sent on mission to our families, friends, colleagues, and coworkers. The practical holiness envisioned by Pope Francis challenges us to boldly stand up to evil, to evangelize others by our words and actions, and to make a mark on the world. Without a sense of mission, we are stunted Christians, our spiritual lives spinning their wheels and going nowhere.

A Family Affair

Over the past ten years, I've encountered people who self-identify as spiritual but not religious. As a result of the clerical sex abuse crisis, church corruption, and religious extremism, they have rejected—sometimes in justifiable anger, sometimes in rightful disgust, and sometimes in demoralized despair—organized religion with its communal prayers, liturgies, and celebrations. They express their spiritual devotion through private forms of spirituality that can include traditional Christian prayer, but also yoga, healing stones, meditation, Qigong, astrology, or even walking in a museum at times when they used to attend religious services. They join virtual groups that require neither responsibility nor commitment and use apps that promote mindfulness and prayer—as hermits disconnected from any community. They have transformed the spiritual journey into a solitary and individual affair.

Pope Francis offers us a spirituality of community as his fourth sign of contemporary holiness. "Growth in holiness is a journey in community, side by side with others" (141). He gives six examples of groups, five of whom were martyrs possessing *parrhesia*, who became blessed or saints in community. Though he only mentions them in passing, let's take a closer look at each of the six groups.

In the thirteenth century, seven noblemen of Florence, a city torn by political strife and riddled with a heresy that professed all physical reality as inherently evil, withdrew from the city to a solitary place for prayer and a life dedicated to God. Because their life of penance and prayer was disturbed by a steady stream of visitors from the city, they sought deeper solitude on the slopes of Mount Senario. Under the direction of a Dominican preacher, they donned a black religious habit, lived according to the Rule of St. Augustine, and adopted the name "Servants of Mary." The seven holy founders of the Order of the Servants of Mary lived a more mendicant than monastic life and were canonized in 1888.

In early 1936, during the Spanish Civil War when religious persecution was intense, most of the Sisters of the Visitation in Madrid moved over two hundred miles to Oronoz. They left a group of six nuns under the direction of Sr. Maria Gabriela de Hinojosa. By July, these seven nuns were confined to an apartment. A neighbor reported them to the authorities and in early November the apartment was searched. The nuns, telling their caretaker that if their deaths could save Spain they were willing to become martyrs, refused to seek refuge in a consulate. On the evening of November 18, a patrol of the Iberian Anarchist Federation broke into the apartment and ordered the seven nuns to leave. They were taken by van to a vacant area and shot. Sr. Maria Cecilia, who had managed to escape, surrendered shortly after and was shot five days later on the outskirts of Madrid. The seven nuns were beatified in 1998.

The pontiff looks to Asia for two more examples of groups canonized as saints. He mentions the sixteenth-century Japanese Jesuit seminarian Paul Miki and his twenty-five companions. Franciscan missionaries went to Japan from the Philippines at the request of Spain's King Philip II. Their presence upset a delicate balance between the Church and the Japanese authorities. When a Spanish ship was seized off the Japanese coast and found to be carrying artillery, suspicions against Catholic missionaries grew. An imperial minister responded by sentencing twenty-six Catholics to death by crucifixion and lancing, after walking them six hundred miles from Kyoto to Nagasaki. The group consisted of three Japanese Jesuits, six foreign Franciscans, and a group of Japanese laity that included children. United in their works of charity and evangelization, the martyrs of Japan were beatified in 1627 and canonized in 1862.

The second example from Asia are the Korean martyrs Andrew Kim Taegon and his companions. During the nineteenth century, Catholics in Korea were persecuted by the ruling Joseon Dynasty for abandoning Confucianism. The martyrdom of his father inspired fifteen-year-old Andrew Kim Taegon to travel to faraway Macao and study for the priesthood. After his ordination in Shanghai, the Christian community helped this first native-born priest to secretly reenter the country and were overjoyed to have him celebrate the sacraments. In 1846 at the age of twenty-five, after a failed attempt to smuggle French missionaries into Korea, Andrew Kim Taegon was arrested and put to death for his faith. Between 1839 and 1867, one hundred and three Catholics were martyred. They were men and women, young and old, peasant and wealthy. In 1984, Pope John Paul II traveled to South Korea and, breaking with the tradition of a canonization ceremony only occurring at the Vatican, canonized the martyrs of Korea on their native soil.

Pope Francis looks to South America for yet another example of martyrdom and holiness in community. Seventeenth-century Spanish conquistadors in Paraguay were enslaving the native peoples of the land. Roque Gonzalez helped them become self-sufficient and free. As a Jesuit, he helped found the "reductions," independent, self-governing, and self-supporting tribal communities that excluded European settlers. He and other Jesuits built more than thirty reductions with an average population of three thousand in each. In 1628, Roque Gonzalez and confreres Alonso Rodriguez and Juan de Castillo started a reduction along the Iijui River. This roused the hostility of a medicine man who lost his local influence and decided to kill the Jesuits. On November 15, his men tomahawked Roque Gonzalez and Alonso Rodriguez. Two days later, they stoned Juan de Castillo to death. In 1988, these three Jesuits became the first American martyrs to be canonized.

The seven Trappist monks of Tibhirine, Algeria, are the final group of future saints whom the pontiff explicitly mentions as finding holiness together in community. This community of nine monks knew they were in danger and likely would be killed if they remained in Algeria, a country divided by war between Islamic extremist rebels and Algerian government forces. In 1993, the prior of the small monastery had written in a letter that he and the other monks would willingly offer themselves as a sacrifice for the Algerian people. Their work among the people was too important to be abandoned, no matter the circumstances. He added, "When the time comes, I would like to be able to have that stroke of lucidity which would permit me to ask forgiveness of God and of my brothers in humanity, forgiving wholeheartedly, at the same time, whoever my killer might be." On March 27, 1996, a group of twenty armed men stormed the monastery and kidnapped seven of the monks. Two monks, hiding in separate rooms, were left behind. The seven were beheaded two months later. Though it is unclear if they were killed by the Islamic extremists or died by accident in a failed rescue mission by the army, Pope Francis declared them martyrs in January 2018. Their story was depicted in the 2010 French drama *Of Gods and Men.*

A medieval community of men in Italy. A twentieth-century community of sisters in Spain. A sixteenth-century group of Japanese Catholics who walked to their martyrdom. Nineteenth-century martyrs of Korea, many of whom did not know one another, but whose witness and stories inspired each other. Three seventeenth-century Jesuits in South America with the zeal of contemporary social activists. Seven French Trappist monks who prepared as a community for martyrdom in Northern Africa. Different people from different times and countries. Yet, these are all poignant, dramatic, and perennial examples of how God's grace transforms people into saints not in isolation but through interaction with others.

In Marriage and Relationships

This transformation is not confined to martyrdom, nor to vowed religious. The pontiff's practical holiness includes the sacrament of marriage, where "each spouse becomes a means used by Christ for the sanctification of the other" (141). I instantly thought of Louis and Zélie Martin, the parents of Thérèse of Liseiux, who were canonized in October 2015. He studied to become a religious priest but couldn't learn Latin; she entered the convent but soon discerned it was not God's will. They met, married, and initially decided to live together as celibates. But a wise priest convinced them to be open to children—and children they had, nine of them! In their lives together with the joys and struggles of raising their daughters, Louis and Zélie Martin were transformed into holy people.

Every day I see examples such as this around me. For example, Pat and Charlie are unable to have children, but that doesn't keep them from being open to life. Pat is a volunteer Sunday school teacher at her church; Charlie is a coach for a neighborhood Little League baseball team. After twenty years of marriage, they are still very much in love and often display their mutual affection in public. People at their church think of them as outstanding examples of Christian disciples—but the couple is aware they need one another to be just that. "He's always encouraging me," Pat says. "She keeps me on the straight and narrow," Charlie confides. No wonder God states, "It is not good that the man should be alone; I will make him a helper as his partner" (Gen 2:18).

People often bring their struggles in relationships to spiritual direction. One might have issues with a spouse. Another might be disappointed in an adult child. One religious sister might have a personality conflict with a community member. A priest might have challenges with his bishop or his parish council president. In each and every case, God's grace is at work, not despite the challenging person, but precisely *in* the relationship with the person. Pope Francis quotes John of the Cross's words to one of his Carmelite confreres, "You are living with others in order to be fashioned and tried" (141).

When are you tempted to withdraw from a relationship? When does the cloud of frustration hinder you from seeing and holding the other's hand? Do you know that temptation and frustration can signal a moment of grace you are resisting? Rather than retreat and withdraw, bring the situation to prayer. Describe the entire situation to God. Then wait and ponder.

As you ponder the tension in your relationship or the nuisance the other person is, ask yourself three simple questions: *What is God saying to me in this relationship? What issues does this relationship or this person bring up in me? How is God speaking to me in this frustration?*

Your withdrawal, resistance, and frustration can be indications of unresolved issues:

- Are you too proud to stand in obedience to another person?
- Do you insist upon controlling the other person or manipulating the situations that God sends?
- Do you lack the basic self-confidence and self-acceptance required in adult relationships?

Psychological issues of authority, control, and self-image are critical aspects of your spiritual life that touch on how you relate to God and often reveal your understanding of detachment, surrender, and acceptance; they also can indicate where you might need to grow in a healthy love of self. It's appropriate to discuss these issues with a spiritual director. Why? Because God's grace might be calling you to open wider the door of your heart to psychological fitness and spiritual growth. Holiness does not consist in psychological perfection and wholeness; we never become "superhuman" (50) as Pope Francis reminded us in chapter two, but we embark on a slow and progressive walk beyond the ego.

The Mysticism of One-on-One

Sharing faith, God's word, and celebrating the Eucharist with others are communal practices of holiness that "make us a holy and missionary community" and can give rise "to authentic and shared mystical experiences" (142). The pope makes passing reference to the stories of Saints Scholastica and Benedict as well as Saints Augustine and Monica.

The Benedictine tradition states that Saints Scholastica and Benedict were twins, and that she would annually visit with her brother. Benedict would leave his cell and visit his sister outside the monastery's gate, where they would pray together and talk about the spiritual life. Once, Scholastica complained that their annual visit had flown by too quickly. She begged her brother to stay a while longer, but Benedict refused, saying he was not allowed to be absent from his cell overnight. Scholastica then prayed to God asking for a reason for her twin to stay. Suddenly, a flash of lightning, a clap of thunder, and pouring rain made it impossible for Benedict to return. With the answer to her prayer, Scholastica and Benedict spent the night in continued holy conversation and found spiritual fulfillment in their relationship with one another.

In the case of Saints Augustine and his mother Monica, Pope Francis quotes a famous passage from Book IX of Augustine's *Confessions* that highlights how friendship and companionship can lead us to a shared mystical experience. Shortly before her death in 387, Monica and Augustine leaned into a window that looked into a garden and shared an experience of God in Ostia. Augustine described their experience as opening their hearts to God and having an intellectual insight into eternal life. Clearly this shared experience was partly emotional, partly intellectual, and powerful enough to free Monica from the constraints she had to the physical world. No longer was she concerned about where or with whom she would be buried. Soon afterward, Monica died and Augustine mourned her death.

Though the pope doesn't mention it, a Franciscan legend about Saints Francis and Clare offers yet another incident of a shared mystical experience. Francis had continually turned down Clare's request to share a meal. Some friars finally persuaded him, saying, "Divine charity demands it. After all, she renounced her possessions when she accepted your preaching." A meeting and a meal were arranged at the little church of St. Mary of the Angels, located in the woods outside the city walls.

At the appointed hour, the saints, each with companions, met and sat on the ground. As they ate, Francis began to speak about God in such a marvelous and mystical way that he himself, Clare, and the companions were caught up in God.

Meanwhile, horror seized the citizens of Assisi as they watched from a distance the little church and the entire forest around it go up in flames. The citizens rushed down the hill with buckets of water and hearts spilling over with the hope of extinguishing the fire. Upon arrival at the church, they found Francis, Clare, and the companions rapt in mystical ecstasy.

And the fire? There was none. The blaze the people saw was the fire of divine love burning in the lives of these simple followers of Christ. The people of Assisi returned home greatly consoled and edified.

The legend as well as the stories of Saint Benedict and Saint Augustine remind us that sharing faith and God's word, as well as our friendship, offers spiritual nourishment and inspiration to others. But you don't have to reach back to history or legend to discover that. Some people are eager to share how soul friends and spouses, by word and deed, inspire, encourage, and embolden them to live authentic holy lives. I have often heard a husband confess, "It's my wife and her faith that pull me along on the spiritual journey." And many a vowed religious will look at someone in community and whisper, "He inspired me," or "She taught me by her own life." We sometimes forget how God uses others as instruments of grace for our own spiritual growth—and how we might unknowingly be an inspiration for others.

The Angel in the Details

Shared spiritual experiences are not the most frequent or important when it comes to practical holiness. Pope Francis favors an ordinary approach like Thérèse of Lisieux's "Little Way." "The common life, whether in the family, the parish, the religious community or any other, is made up of small everyday things" (143). Referring to Gospel incidents and parables, the pontiff highlights how Jesus asked his disciples to pay attention to details:

- that wine was running out at a marriage feast (John 2:1–12);
- a sheep went missing (Matt. 18:12–14; Lk. 15:3–7);
- a poor widow contributed two small coins to the treasury (Lk. 21:1–4);
- the extra oil brought along for lamps, should the bridegroom delay (Matt. 25:1–13);
- asking the number of loaves of bread brought into the desert (Matt. 14:13–21; Mk. 6:31–44; Lk. 9:12–17; John 6:1–14);
- having breakfast prepared on the beach (John 21:1–14).

It's in a community's practice of the little details of love—in footnote 107 Pope Francis notes the importance of saying "please," "thank you," and "sorry" in a timely fashion—that the risen Lord is present, blessing the community according to the Father's plan.

A few years ago, the Poor Clares of Memphis, Tennessee, asked me to give a three-day workshop on St. Clare of Assisi. Fearing that the women, who lived the very contemplative life Clare envisioned, would know more than me, I decided to focus on the testimony of the witnesses interviewed during Clare's canonization process. What did they observe about the potential saint? I was stunned to discover that none of the witnesses spoke of the future saint's prayer or mystical experiences. Instead, they spoke of the foundress's humility, patience, charity, and kindness. They mentioned how she gently and carefully handed them water and covered them at night. They spoke of her little silent touches when she woke them for prayer. The witnesses admired Clare's care and attentive compassion for their needs, problems, struggles, and temptations. In her attention to these little details of love, Clare became an ecclesial model for domestic holiness.

This is the challenge of living in a religious community—and maybe you've discovered it in your family life as well. The sin of entitlement seems prevalent everywhere: I leave the dirty dish on the kitchen table, knowing someone else will rinse it and put it in the dishwasher. I don't think to say "please" when asking for the salt and pepper. I irritate a confrere and hesitate to apologize. It's easy to forget common courtesies and the little details of love—the call to domestic holiness—when you live daily with the same group of men or women, or in a family.

Pope Francis concludes his reflection on the communal aspect of contemporary holiness by turning to the Carmelite tradition and reminding us that God sometimes offers consolation as we attend to the small details of love. Again, he cites Thérèse of Lisieux.

A little background to the quote: Thérèse was given the responsibility of taking care of elderly, crochety Sister St. Pierre. Sometimes accepting insults for walking too fast or too slow or being too young to help, the future saint would help the nun walk to the refectory and once there, turn up the sleeves of St. Pierre's habit so the elderly nun could eat without soiling her religious garb. Thérèse did all this without complaint and even with kindness. Over time, she noticed Sister St. Pierre struggling to cut her bread, so Thérèse helped her and left with a smile. She gradually won over the elderly nun.

Once, while helping Sister St. Pierre, Thérèse heard a musical instrument off in the distance. She imagined a gilded parlor filled with finely dressed young ladies chatting and complimenting each other. Suddenly, her attention was drawn back to grumpy old Sister St. Pierre and her cacophony of complaints—and God instantly illumined the saint's soul with the light of truth. This moment of mystical consolation unfolded in the middle of a small act of charity. That's the story behind the quote in paragraph 145:

> One winter night I was carrying out my little duty as usual. . . . Suddenly, I heard off in the distance the harmonious sound of a musical instrument. I then pictured a well-lighted drawing room, brilliantly gilded, filled with elegantly dressed young ladies conversing together and conferring upon each other all sorts of compliments and other worldly remarks. Then my glance fell upon the poor invalid whom I was supporting. Instead of the beautiful strains of music I heard only her occasional complaints. . . . I cannot express in words what happened in my soul; what I know is that the Lord illumined it with rays of truth which so surpassed the dark brilliance of earthly feasts that I could not believe my happiness.

A Short Course on Prayer

Pope Francis is clear about the fifth and final sign of holiness in today's world: "I do not believe in holiness without prayer, even though that prayer need not be lengthy or involve intense emotions" (147). To know that one doesn't have to pray for two hours a day like the Missionaries of Charity founded by Mother Teresa of Calcutta, or be caught up in ecstatic experiences of God's presence like some medieval visionary, is a great comfort to me, and it indicates once again the practical holiness promoted by the pope.

For each disciple, it is essential to spend time with the Master, to listen to his words, and to learn from him always. Unless we listen, all our words will be nothing but useless chatter. (150)

Prayer's aim is to make us prayerful: to remain always in the presence of God, and with that awareness to go about the chores and obligations of our day. Fostering that awareness—what Francis of Assisi called "the spirit of prayer and devotion"—requires spending some moments alone with God. And the pontiff hints that this is easier than we might think, as he uses Teresa of Avila's definition of prayer as "nothing but friendly intercourse, and frequent solitary converse, with him who we know loves us." Returning again to the importance of opening one's heart, the pope continues, "Trust-filled prayer is a response of a heart open to encountering God face to face, where all is peaceful and the quiet voice of the Lord can be heard in the midst of silence" (149). It is from that encounter and in that silence—which is not "a form of escape and rejection of the world" (152)—that "we can discern, in the light of the Spirit, the paths of holiness to which the Lord is calling us" (150).

Basking in the Gaze of Jesus, Entering His Heart and Wounds

Not only do we discover our particular mission as we contemplate the face of Jesus but also we are healed of the brokenness caused by our struggles and sins. It gave me cause to pause when I read the line, "We must not domesticate the power of the face of Christ." Pope Francis immediately turns his attention to the reader and asks, "Are there moments when you place yourself quietly in the Lord's presence, when you calmly spend time with him, when you bask in his gaze? Do you let his fire inflame your heart?" (151)

Pause and consider your answer to the pope's questions. It's important that we do this because holiness includes spending time alone with Jesus and allowing him to stir into flame the smoldering ashes in our lives.

By allowing the divine gaze to warm us with love, we catch fire—and then we are able to set others on fire by our words and witness. Note the connection between prayer and mission. Prayer is not a static encounter or some form of navel gazing but a divine stoking of the heart whose sparks (our words and actions) affect others. The effect of a saint's prayer is never individual or solitary—it is communal.

For those of us too broken to encounter Jesus face-to-face, the pontiff draws upon the suggestion of the twelfth-century founder of the Cistercians, Bernard of Clairvaux, and offers a piece of advice: "If, gazing on the face of Christ, you feel unable to let yourself be healed and transformed, then enter into the Lord's heart, into his wounds, for that is the abode of divine mercy" (151).

This devotion to the heart and wounds of Christ has a rich tradition dating back to the earliest days of the Church. It was developed by Augustine and flowered in the twelfth century. But how does one express this ancient devotion today? What exactly does Pope Francis mean when he invites us to "enter into" the heart and wounds of Christ?

A number of years ago, I was working through the emotional damage left behind by my father's suicide.

I was too angry at God and emotionally scarred to look Christ in the face. I distinctly remember avoiding looking at crucifixes or even reading the Bible. When I told my spiritual director about my anger and the guilt that came with avoiding Christ at any cost, he looked at me and gently said, "Sometimes you have to go through the side door."

"The side door?" I asked.

"Yes, the side door. Sometimes all we can do is lean against Jesus without saying anything. Think of a little boy who had his feelings hurt for the first time. He doesn't know what to do or what he is feeling so he just gets in the chair with his father and lets his father hold him.

"Picture yourself in the heart of Jesus—you don't have to look at him or say anything. Just sit there like that little boy and breathe in Christ's understanding, mercy, and compassion. The whole point is to recognize that Jesus himself knows the pain and anguish we sometimes suffer. And so we enter his wounds and sit in his heart. We let our emotional pain and physical suffering *be* the very words we can't pray. Our trauma or guilt becomes the glance we dare not raise."

Sadly, many of us think prayer is something that goes on from the neck up with eyes raised. But a downward glance sometimes is the heart's cry—prayer—for an inner healing. This simple method of entering Christ's wounds and heart honors that.

Praying Your Life

Prayer does not happen in a vacuum or a hermetically sealed container—the pope states explicitly that it should not be "unalloyed contemplation of God, free of all distraction, as if the names and faces of others were somehow an intrusion to be avoided" (154). Rather, ours is a God who entered history, "and so our prayer is interwoven with memories. We think back not only to his revealed Word, but also on our own lives, the lives of others, and all that the Lord has done in his Church" (153). This gives birth to a grateful memory as we become mindful of the blessings, love, and mercy we have received from God. By praying over even "the smallest details" (153) of our lives, we discover how God has never forgotten us. Remember Carlita's story earlier in this chapter?

Pope Francis writes briefly about the prayers of supplication, petition, and intercession. Supplication, as a plea for personal help, proclaims our trust, faith-filled love, and great confidence in God as well as our inability to do anything on our own. Petition, the request for something desired, "calms our hearts and helps us persevere in hope." Of particular value is intercession, petitions on behalf of others, because it is not only an act of trust but also an expression of love for our neighbor: "Intercessory prayer is an expression of our fraternal concern for others, since we are able to embrace their lives, their deepest troubles and their loftiest dreams" (154); clearly it is not, as some view it, a rain dance that opens up the heavens when done long enough and correctly.

Love Pauses

When introducing the prayer of adoration, the pontiff quotes a letter written by Charles de Foucauld in 1901: "As soon as I believed that there was a God, I understood that I could do nothing other than to live for him" (155).

Who was Charles de Foucauld? He was born into an aristocratic French family in 1858. At the age of 32, he became a Trappist monk, first in France and then at Akbès on the Syrian-Turkish border. After seven years, he left the monastery to lead a solitary life of prayer near a Poor Clare convent in Nazareth. In 1901, after ordination to the priesthood in Viviers, France, he took up residence in French Algeria, where he lived an eremitical life. First settling in Béni Abbès, near the Moroccan border, he later moved to share the life and challenges of the Tuareg people, in Tamanghasset in southern Algeria. It was here that he came up with the idea of founding a new religious community called the Little Brothers of Jesus. He never saw that community come into existence. In late 1916, de Foucauld was murdered after a failed kidnapping attempt. He was beatified as a martyr in 2005.

Pope Francis says the realization of the existence of God leads us to share in de Foucauld's dedication. We want to worship and adore God "at times in quiet wonder, and praise him in festive song" (155).

Drawing from the 2007 *Aparecida Document* of the Latin American and Caribbean bishops, the pope offers a simple, practical method of adoring God. Turn your attention to something that represents God's love and closeness to you. Perhaps it's a favorite statue, a freshly cut flower from your garden, or a photograph of your spouse and children. Keep your gaze fixed upon the object, open the door of your heart, and allow God's presence conveyed by the object to touch you. You're not actively doing anything but surrendering to God's presence. "Love pauses, contemplates the mystery, and enjoys it in silence" (155). This is the kind of contemplation Charles de Foucauld practiced as a hermit.

The pope concludes his reflections on prayer reminding us of the integral connection between praying with Scripture and the celebration of the Eucharist. In Scripture we hear the voice of the Master and discover a light for our path. The pontiff cites the bishops of India, who remind us that scriptural prayer is not simply "one of many devotions, beautiful but somewhat optional" but "goes to the very heart and identity of Christian life" and "has the power to transform lives" (156).

How can we discover our identity in Scripture? How can we experience its transformative power? There's a traditional method of scriptural prayer, called *lectio divina* ("divine reading"), that can help us do both. Designed by a twelfth-century Carthusian monk, this method continues to be practiced by twenty-first-century Christians. It consists of four steps:

- *Read.* Familiarize yourself with the chosen passage by reading it two or three times. Don't forget to read the biblical editor's footnotes, because they will sometimes help you understand the context and meaning of the passage.
- *Reflect.* Ponder what you've just read. Perhaps it jogs a memory. Sit with a word or verse that jumps off the page—it's trying to tell you something. Medieval writers used to suggest "chewing" on this text like a cow chews its cud. Or roll the text around in your

heart as if it were fine wine rolling around in your mouth. The text might add some information to your intellect or evoke an emotion from your heart.

- *Pray.* Tell God why this passage was surprising, uplifting, challenging, or convicting. Perhaps you feel prompted to say a prayer of praise, contrition, intercession, or petition.

- *Contemplate.* Sit in the holy silence of God's presence that follows your prayer. Bask in God's love.

Contemporary authors sometimes make explicit a fifth step:

- *Act.* Having read, pondered, and prayed over the Word of God, commit to enfleshing its meaning or message by the way you think, speak, and act. This is how Scripture can change our lives, as the bishops of India remind us. The Letter of James states it this way: It is not enough to be students of the Scripture, "But be doers of the word, and not merely hearers who deceive themselves" (James 1:22).

Pope Francis reminds us of a spiritual chain reaction that brings together the written Word, the living Word, and the transformation called holiness: "Meeting Jesus in the Scriptures leads us to the Eucharist," which is the greatest worship of God, for it is God's very Son who is offered; "When we receive him in Holy Communion, we renew our covenant with him and allow him to carry out ever more fully his work of transforming our lives" (157). Receiving the Eucharist requires opening the door of the heart and giving God the opportunity to change our thoughts, desires, and actions.

This chapter of *Rejoice and Be Glad* invites us to look in the mirror and ask ourselves five important questions:

- Am I rooted in God, who graces me with perseverance, patience, and humility?
- Am I bold and passionate about my faith and my mission, never fearing to walk to the fringes of society?
- Am I positive, hopeful, and joyful?
- Do I actively embrace relationships and pay attention to their details?
- Am I prayerful?

The answers to these questions, based on the "five great expressions of love for God and neighbor" (111), will tell us whether or not the door of our heart is open to grace.

REFLECTION QUESTIONS

1. Which of the five signs of holiness comfort you? Challenge you? How do they find expression in your life?

2. Practice the "methodless method" of God's abiding presence promoted by Brother Lawrence of the Resurrection. Sit comfortably in a chair and for fifteen minutes, imagine God's grace-filled presence as the air you breathe. When you are finished, reflect on your experience and reaction to this practice.

3. Revisit the ten safe havens of complacency. Which ones resonate in your life? What can you do to move beyond them?

CHAPTER FIVE

Spiritual Combat, Vigilance, and Discernment

"The Christian life is a constant battle" (158). This opening sentence of *Gaudete et Exsultate*'s fifth chapter jogged a memory.

A few years ago, I was giving a workshop on some basic principles of the spiritual life. When I spoke about the challenge of surrendering our desires and accepting the will of God, I used an image that comes naturally and spontaneously to many men: "Think of the spiritual life as a battle. And, surprisingly, defeat *is* victory! Every day and each situation challenge us to lay down our weapons, to die to ourselves, and to let God take over—or, paraphrasing the words of John the Baptist, 'Decreasing ourselves so God can increase.'"

As I continued, a woman raised her hand. I acknowledged it.

"I'm a bit uncomfortable, Father, with your military imagery. That hasn't been my experience at all." A whispered *y-e-s* ricocheted through the room as some women nodded. "I think of the spiritual life as a relationship. My challenge is not to lay down my weapons and be defeated—but to surrender ever more deeply to the grace of God and pray Mary's 'Fiat. Let it be done to me as you say.' It's like offering hospitality to God and inviting him to my table—but *he's* the cook, not me. My struggle is with the resistance to that surrender and to the food he has prepared."

This was an illuminating comment that stopped me in my tracks. Then I laughed at my ignorance. It had never dawned on me that men and women could look at the spiritual life from such different perspectives.

Spiritual Combat

Can Pope Francis, with his military image for the spiritual life, be a helpful spiritual companion for women as well as men? Can his male perspective be applicable to a feminine understanding of a relationship with God? I think so. Though men and women might use different images and analogies to describe them, the challenges, struggles, and temptations of the spiritual life remain the same. The pontiff mentions three of them: the world and its mentality, our human weaknesses and sinful inclinations, and the devil.

Both men and women know the temptations of the world. Throughout the apostolic exhortation, we have been reminded of the seduction of advertising, commercialism, and the digital world. They tempt and distract us with power, prestige, possessions, and pleasure. We think entertainment and the avoidance of pain make for the good life. We can easily fall into the "culture of zapping" (167) that not only sidetracks us to multiple computer screens and different virtual scenarios, but also keeps us isolated and alone. We need to resist any worldly mentality that fixates the attention on ourselves and neglects our missionary outreach of love and service to others.

We all have imperfections, shortcomings, and weaknesses that keep our hearts closed to grace and lead us down dark alleys, where, on our better days, we prefer not to go. The pope explicitly mentions "laziness, lust, envy, jealousy or any others" (159). Real or perceived childhood deprivations give rise to our adult fixations, compulsions, and sometimes addictions, which can potentially lead us to commit sin. Some of these sins are what I call "default sins"—done on auto-pilot, out of habit, without thought or premeditation.

Remember: The Devil

It is "the devil, the prince of evil" (159) who presents the greatest threat. But who is the devil?

Cf. Paul VI, *Catechesis*, General Audience of 15 November 1972: . . . "Evil is not simply a deficiency, it is an efficiency, a living spiritual being, perverted and perverting. A terrible reality, mysterious and frightful. They no longer remain within the framework of biblical and ecclesiastical teaching who refuse to recognize its existence, or who make of it an independent principle that does not have, like every creature, its origin in God, or explain it as a pseudo-reality, a conceptual and imaginative personification of the hidden causes of our misfortunes." (footnote 121)

A spiritual directee once revealed to me a level of sophistication that I found surprising. "Oh, I have a Master's degree in theology and don't believe in that red-skinned, horned weasel with a pitchfork and a tail. The idea makes for interesting works of art like Michelangelo

Buonarroti's *The Torment of Saint Anthony* that depicts the desert father being attacked by demons on every side—but let's face it, that's a medieval figment and not reality." After reading his apostolic exhortation, I can easily picture Pope Francis raising an eyebrow over such a comment.

Don't let that traditional image—a red-skinned, horned weasel with a pitchfork and a tail—fool you. The pontiff reminds us that the devil is not "a myth, a representation, a symbol, a figure of speech or an idea" (161). He is a "malign power" (160) who "poisons us with the venom of hatred, desolation, envy and vice" (161). Referring to the final petition of the Lord's prayer, "deliver us from evil," the pope writes, "That final word does not refer to evil in the abstract; a more exact translation would be 'the evil one'. It indicates a personal being who assails us. Jesus taught us to ask daily for deliverance from him, lest his power prevail over us" (161).

Because men tend to gravitate toward the idea of spiritual combat, the devil is viewed as the enemy. We need to struggle and fight against him. But how do some women view the devil?

During a break between my lectures, I asked that very question of the woman who had taught me the feminine relationship model for the spiritual life. I found her reply insightful: "I think of Satan as a jilted lover after an acrimonious breakup. He'll do anything to hinder or disrupt my relationship with my newfound lover, God. He'll also try to obstruct my relationships with my family, friends, and the wider community. I need to keep my guard up, because he is merciless in tempting me with varied, sneaky, and insidious devices and designs."

Whether the devil is our enemy or a jilted lover, we have "powerful weapons" (162) given by God to help us resist Satan's attacks and deceitful manipulation. Let me briefly reflect on the eight mentioned by the pope:

- *Faith-filled prayer*: It helps us remain rooted in God and offers us perseverance and patience. Those two qualities build up both our armor and our resistance to the seductions of the prince of darkness.

- *Meditation on the word of God*: This practice gives us insights into the devil's history with humanity, reminds us of Satan's ultimate defeat, and offers us ways to renounce temptations. Scripture's words can be used as retorts and responses to the devil's devious seductions, as Jesus teaches us in his own desert temptations (cf. Matt. 4:1–11; Lk. 4:1–13).

- *The celebration of Mass*: The Eucharistic celebration makes Jesus present in word and sacrament, gives us encouragement and strength, and nourishes us for the spiritual journey.

- *Eucharistic adoration*: The Eucharistic presence of the Risen Christ is a stunning reminder that Satan is ultimately powerless. Opening the door of our hearts to the sacramental presence of Christ emboldens us to continue relying upon divine grace and to rejoice in the Lord's triumph in our lives.

- *Sacramental Reconciliation*: We recognize our weakness in defeating and standing up to the devil. Self-awareness of our failings has its unique rewards. We renew our commitment to be faithful disciples of the Divine Master.

- *Works of charity*: The triumph of love is the bane of the devil. "Above all, maintain constant love for one another, for love covers a multitude of sins" (1 Pet. 4:8). "[A]nd whoever gives even a cup of cold water to one of these little ones in the name of a disciple— truly I tell you, none of these will lose their reward" (Matt. 10:42).

- *Community life*: Pope Francis had mentioned in chapter four, "When we live apart from others, it is very difficult to fight against concupiscence, the snares and temptations of the devil and the selfishness of the world. Bombarded as we are by so many enticements, we can grow too isolated, lose our sense of reality and inner clarity, and easily succumb" (140). There is strength in numbers.

- *Missionary outreach*: This practice keeps the muscles of the heart from atrophying as we move to the fringes of society where Jesus is present in the poor and marginalized. It provides an antidote to mediocrity and complacency.

The pontiff quotes the words of the priest and saint Cura Brochero, who reminds us how careless people are easily seduced by the false, deceptive, and poisonous promises of the devil. Affectionately known as the "Gaucho priest" because he traveled long distances in Argentina on the back of a mule wearing a sombrero and poncho, the late nineteenth-century Jose Gabriel del Rosario Brochero ministered extensively to the poor and sick. On the occasion of his beatification in 2013, Pope Francis wrote to the bishops of Argentina, "He never stayed in the parish office, he got on his mule and went out to find people like a priest of the street—to the point of getting leprosy." Brochero truly had the "smell of the sheep." Leprous, blind, and deaf, he died in early 1914 and was canonized a saint in October 2016.

Getting Below the Surface with Awareness

No matter the causes of our sins—the world and its mentality, our human weaknesses, or the devil—we need strategies for remaining vigilant. Pope Francis writes about keeping "our lamps lit (*Lk.* 12:35) and be[ing] attentive." He cites Jesus, "Keep awake (*Mt* 24:42; *Mk* 13:35)", and Paul, "Let us not fall asleep (*1 Thess* 5:6)" (164). Evangelical pastor Rick Warren, author of the best-selling *The Purpose Driven Life: What on Earth Am I Here For?*, offers one practical way to do just that.

In early June 2018, Warren addressed nearly 800 priests of the Archdiocese of New York on the need to maintain moral integrity. He spoke about the importance of knowing our personal patterns of temptation in order to avoid them. He offered these five questions for reflection:

- *When am I most tempted?* There are moments when my guard is down and I am weak and inclined to sin. They might arise at a particular time of day or with the appearance of a certain feeling like anger, fatigue, or depression.
- *Where am I most tempted?* I probably have a history with some places like bars, hotel rooms, or cities where no one knows me. Or it might be an empty house or sitting alone in my car.

- *Who is with me when I am most tempted?* My temptations might arise when I am alone. Or maybe there are certain acquaintances, friends, or colleagues who use peer pressure to entice and seduce me to join them in sinning—I call those people my "sin sidekicks."
- *What temporary benefit do I get if I give in?* I give in to temptation because there is a payoff involved, usually in the form of a kickback: I feel momentary pleasure; I forget my problems or a feeling I deem inappropriate; I satisfy my lopsided sense of justice.
- *How do I feel right before I am tempted?* My temptation sometimes is the result of an intense feeling that either commands attention and action (like anger, loneliness, frustration, envy, or fear)—or that I deem improper and don't want to feel (like shame, confusion, or loneliness).

These questions make us spiritual investigative reporters getting below the surface of our sins and discovering the times and places we are most vulnerable to the devil's devices, seductions, and temptations. That revelation raises our level of self-awareness and vigilance. Forewarned is forearmed.

Without that self-awareness and vigilance, we might begin thinking we are sinless or even incapable of sinning in the eyes of God. Either thought makes us lethargic and lukewarm, leading to what Pope Francis calls "spiritual corruption." He defines this as "a comfortable and self-satisfied form of blindness. Everything then appears acceptable: deception, slander, egotism and other subtle forms of self-centeredness, for 'even Satan disguises himself as an angel of light' (*2 Cor* 11:14)." In a comment that surprised me, he notes spiritual corruption "is worse than the fall of a sinner" (165). He contrasts an Old Testament father and son to explain: David and Solomon.

David was a young shepherd who, after the deaths of King Saul and his son Jonathan in battle, was anointed king. He sinned by committing adultery with Uriah the Hittite's wife, Bathsheba, and then arranging Uriah's death. However, when confronted by the prophet Nathan, David repented of his sins. After a failed coup by his third son, Absalom, David returned to rule Israel from Jerusalem, where he died peacefully. As the pope notes, ". . . David, who sinned greatly, was able to make up for disgrace" (165).

Not so in the case of one of David's sons born of Bathsheba, Solomon, who followed David as king. Known for his wisdom and initial love of the Lord, Solomon gradually fell prey to self-deception that led to his spiritual corruption. He deliberately violated the Lord's covenant in three ways: he took multiple foreign wives who not only turned his heart to their national deities but also convinced him to build temples to these false gods; he collected a large number of horses and chariots, thus betraying his lust and belief in human rather than divine power; he amassed for himself an exorbitant amount of gold and silver in taxes. God punished Solomon at his death with the division of the kingdom.

Lest we, like Solomon, fall into a form of blindness, self-deception, and spiritual corruption, we need to know if something comes from God, the mentality of the world, or the devil. This leads the pontiff to reflect upon the discernment of spirits, a central theme in his own spirituality as a Jesuit.

"Is This the Will of God?"

A friend comes to me and tells me he is being offered a promotion. It's the position everyone in his IT company would love to have—but it means moving his family to the West Coast and "Something just doesn't feel right about that," he says. "What should I do?"

Katie's mother has been in the hospital for over four months. She's now on life support. The future looks fatal. "It's just a matter of time," Katie says. "As her daughter, I wonder if I should follow the suggestion of the family and take her off life support. . . . What does God want me to do?"

To situations such as these, a spiritual companion like Pope Francis brings an extra pair of ears, knowledge of the spiritual tradition, and the wisdom of experience as we try "to distinguish, separate away, sift off"—the English definition of the Latin *discernere*—God's voice in a chorus of others competing for our heart's attention and response. The practice of discernment is one of the most challenging in the spiritual life, and the pope offers us some sage advice about it. What is discernment? What are its principles? How is it done? When is it necessary? What are its obstacles? I've organized my reflections around those questions and probed this section of the apostolic exhortation for the pontiff's answers.

What is discernment?

An opportunity unexpectedly arises or an issue needs to be addressed: the offer of marriage; the feasibility of moving to another state; the chance to adopt a child; the resolution of an end-of-life issue. How do I know if my decision is the will of God? How can I know if I am being tricked into chasing an illusion or a lie created by my ego, a worldly mentality, or even the devil? In its most basic understanding, Christian discernment is distinguishing and separating away what is of God from that of the world or of the devil.

As a "gift" (166) and "grace" (170), discernment helps us "to recognize the paths that lead to complete freedom"

(168). That freedom is living life to the full: unencumbered by our emotional baggage and immune from our selfish desires, we accept "a call that can shatter our security, but lead us to a better life" (172).

As discernment illumines the path to freedom and we respond to the divine call in the nitty-gritty of our everyday lives, we recognize our God-given mission and the word that God wants to speak through us. We leave ourselves behind "in order to approach the mystery of God, who helps us to carry out the mission to which he has called us, for the good of our brothers and sisters" (175). Discernment is the discovery of our destiny: "It has to do with the meaning of my life before the Father who knows and loves me, with the real purpose of my life, which nobody knows better than he. Ultimately, discernment leads to the wellspring of undying life: to know the Father, the only true God, and the one whom he has sent, Jesus Christ (cf. *Jn* 17:3)" (170).

What are the principles of discernment?

As I pondered the discernment section of *Gaudete et Exsultate*, I unearthed seven principles about discernment. I think each is worth a comment.

1. Discernment is required not only when we stand at a crossroads in life—"when we need to resolve grave problems and make crucial decisions"—but also in the "simple everyday realities" (169) of our responsibilities

and commitments. We open our hearts to grace and ask ourselves constantly, "What is God saying to me in this person, this situation, this feeling, or this thought?" This reflective lifestyle is a valuable aid in coming to know the promptings of God and the invitations to growth.

2. Timing is everything. In two paragraphs, Pope Francis refers to God's "timetable" (169, 174). Without daily reflection, it's easy to miss the opportune call of God, the offer of grace, and the transformation of holiness that accompanies our response. Asking a child's question about the cookies baking in the oven, "Is it time?", is a worthy spiritual practice.

3. Discernment involves daily awareness and sensitivity to the myriad ways God speaks. It doesn't take special abilities or erudite analysis. The pontiff reminds us, "The Father readily reveals himself to the lowly (cf. *Mt* 11:25)" (170).

The Lord speaks to us in a variety of ways, at work, through others and at every moment. (171)

4. Our life is the megaphone God uses to speak to us. "We must remember that prayerful discernment must be born of a readiness to listen: to the Lord and to others, and to reality itself, which always challenges us in new ways" (172). Think of Mary, who, upon hearing the angel's words reported by the shepherds, "treasured all these words and pondered them in her heart" (Lk. 2:19). Discernment requires the heart's sober reflection upon the facts and feelings of daily living.

5. Unlike our will, God's will does not constrict us within a box or bind us in chains. Just the opposite: It frees us from "rigidity, which has no place before the perennial 'today' of the risen Lord." Because of this freedom, discernment allows the "newness of the Gospel [to] emerge in another light" (173).

6. Discernment requires the patience to allow God to work in God's own time; as my spiritual director likes to remind me, "Don't crawl or race—just follow God's pace." It also requires the generosity to sacrifice and never say no to the Lord's requests; "God asks

everything of us, yet he also gives everything to us. He does not want to enter our lives to cripple or diminish them, but to bring them to fulfillment" (175). Consequently, we are always dissatisfied with our gift to God and constantly strive "for all that is great, better and more beautiful" (169).

7. Discernment is shadowed by the cross. We die to our hopes, dreams, and desires to discover our truest identity and God-given mission. Quoting Bonaventure, Pope Francis reminds us that the thirteenth-century Franciscan theologian pointed to the cross and said, "This is our logic" (174).

Christ mirrored these seven principles. His daily food was to do the will of the Father and to complete his work (cf. John 4:34). He grew in the awareness of God's timetable— "My time has not yet come" (John 2:4, 7:6). He lived a life freed from social and sometimes religious conventions: he ate with public sinners (cf. Lk. 15:2); he didn't practice all the fasting and cleansing rituals of his day (cf. Matt. 9:14; Mk. 7:5; Lk. 7:34); he violated the Sabbath when need or charity demanded (cf. Matt. 12:2; Lk. 13:10–17). In the garden of Gethsemane, he pondered and listened to his life (cf. Lk. 22:42), ultimately sacrificing and giving his all on the cross: "Father, into your hands I commend my spirit"

(Lk. 23:46). That discernment and surrender to the cross would be matched by the Father's decision to raise Jesus from the dead.

How do we discern?

Because discernment is a gift and grace, we cannot presume to have it. Pope Francis reminds us of our role in acquiring it: "If we ask with confidence that the Holy Spirit grant us this gift, and then seek to develop it through prayer, reflection, reading and good counsel, then surely we will grow in this spiritual endowment" (166). Let's take a look at the practical implications of those four practices.

If we live with one eye on our Facebook page and the other checking the maximum characters on Twitter while listening to the latest downloaded podcast on our iPhone, we will be unable to find the road to freedom or know our God-given mission. Many people have difficulty believing this today. As useful as technology is, Pope Francis is reminding us of a practical necessity for our spiritual life: We need *"prolonged prayer"* and the silence it brings. There we learn how "to interpret the real meaning of the inspirations we believe we have received" (171).

The thought that an inspiration might be from God does not necessarily mean it is; as the pontiff, quoting Paul, reminded us in paragraph 165, "[E]ven Satan disguises himself as an angel of light (*2 Cor* 11:14)." The silence of prolonged prayer helps us discern—"to distinguish, separate away, or sift off"—the source of the inspiration; it turns down the volume of our life's cacophony and helps us learn the grammar and syntax of "God's language" (171).

The Carmelite mystic John of the Cross would agree. He famously wrote, "God's first language is silence." I remember hearing Trappist Abbot Thomas Keating continuing this image: "Everything else is a poor translation. In order to understand this language, we must learn to be silent and to rest in God."

This silence then is not empty. It is filled with message and meaning. That's why prolonged prayer includes "a readiness to listen" (172). As a young Franciscan friar, I didn't know how to listen in prayer or even what that meant. Thankfully, a spiritual director helped me.

"See if this image helps: It's early in the morning and you're in the middle of an empty field. You're lying on your back and looking up at the sky. As the different clouds make their way in formation across the sky, what do you see? Do they remind you of anything? Do they bring up any feelings or concerns?

"That's a great analogy for listening in prayer. You sit and call to mind you are surrounded by God. You are 'in God,' as Paul reminds us. As you sit in that divine presence, gently whisper, 'Speak, Lord, your servant is listening.' Then wait

. . . and watch the feelings, thoughts, and memories that form and float across your consciousness. They sometimes will trigger reactions—good, bad, exciting, challenging, frightening, and discouraging ones. The feelings, thoughts, memories, and reactions that bring you closer to God might be an invitation that needs to be opened, discussed, and given a response. The ones that move you away from God could be an illusion or temptation. Bring it all to me for spiritual direction. Through examination and discussion, we'll gradually come to discover the will of God and the role God wants you to play in it."

This sounded complicated and intimidating at first. *God was actually going to speak to me?* I had my doubts—and false starts. But I gradually got the hang of it. After almost thirty-five years, this practice of listening to the silence of prolonged prayer is easier and is reassuring.

The second practice mentioned in paragraph 166 of *Rejoice and Be Glad* that helps us receive the grace and gift of discernment is *reflection*. Pope Francis writes that God "asks us to examine what is within us—our desires, anxieties, fears and questions—and what takes place all around us— 'the signs of the times'—and thus to recognize the paths that lead to complete freedom" (168). The fact that our inner world and outer world go hand-in-hand prevents discernment from becoming an amateur form of self-analysis, some kind of egotistical navel-gazing, or an unconscious reaction to the external situation. Our discerned mission and the word God wants to speak through us often emerge in the very interplay and prayerful pondering of our inner and outer worlds.

The pontiff has a specific request: ". . . I ask all Christians not to omit, in dialogue with the Lord, a sincere daily 'examination of conscience'" (169). That's a time-honored method of spiritual reflection. A Web search will lead to versions of an examination of conscience based on the Ten Commandments, the Beatitudes (a good place to start in light of the third chapter of *Rejoice and Be Glad*), and even Catholic Social Teaching. Let me offer the following based upon the five "great expressions of love for God and neighbor" (111) mentioned in the fourth chapter of the apostolic exhortation.

Spend a few minutes in silence. Take slow, deep breaths to bring yourself back to the present moment. Remind yourself that you are in God's presence. Ask the Holy Spirit to open the door of your heart to divine grace as you make this examination of conscience. When you are ready, gently but honestly ponder three questions chosen at random from each sign of holiness:

Perseverance, Patience, and Meekness

- How did my words and actions today show where I am grounded? Are my roots in the ego, the false trappings of the world, the fascination with the devil, or in God?

- When was my perseverance in doing good tested? How did I respond?

- How did my aggressive and selfish inclinations take root in my words and actions today?

- When did I take part in verbal violence through the Web and the various means of digital communication (social media, etc.)?

- When did I look down on others like a heartless judge?

- What were my humiliations today? How did I surrender and accept them?

- When did I fail to disagree gently? To demand justice? To defend the weak before the powerful? What held me back from speaking up?

Joy and a Sense of Humor

- How did I radiate a joyful, positive, and hopeful spirit today?

- How did I display a sense of humor? How many times did I laugh?

- How was my sadness a sign of ingratitude?

- How did I express gratitude to God today? How many blessings did I receive from God?

Boldness and Passion

- How did I evangelize today? What mark did it leave at the office, in my home, in my neighborhood?
- How was I bold and enthusiastic in speaking about my faith?
- How did I take up Jesus's challenge to put out into the deep and meet him at the very fringes of society?
- What gifts of mine did I put at the service of others today?
- How was I bold, courageous, and compassionate in my mission today?
- How did fear and excessive caution keep me within safe bounds?
- What safe havens (individualism, spiritualism, living in a small world, addiction, intransigence, the rejection of new ideas and approaches, dogmatism, nostalgia, pessimism, hiding behind rules and regulations) did I take refuge in today? Why?
- How was my heart open to my brothers and sisters, their wounded flesh, their troubles, and their profound desolation?
- When did I fall prey to complacency and mediocrity, letting things be? How can I break this habit?

- How would I describe my sense of being a missionary today?

In Community

- Who helped me grow in holiness today?
- How do my spouse, significant other, children, extended family, and friends challenge me to grow in holiness?
- How did I pay attention to the small details of love in my various relationships today?
- How many times did I say "please," "thank you," "I'm sorry" today?
- How many hours did I spend in front of the television and computer screen today? How often did I check my phone? What does that time investment say about me and my lifestyle?
- What patterns of behavior do I see in myself that betray my choice for isolation and individualism over community?

In Constant Prayer

- How was I open to God today? When and how did I pray alone?
- What did God say to me today in prayer, my circumstances, and the people I encountered?
- How and when did I spend time listening to the silence of God's language?

- How did the fire of my prayer life touch others today?
- When did I pray over the smallest details of my life? What did I learn?
- Who and what needs of the world should I remember in my prayer?
- What did I learn from praying with Scripture?
- In my reception of the Eucharist, how did I renew my covenant with Jesus and open the door of my heart to his transforming grace?

Once you have finished, in light of your responses, spend a few minutes asking how today's words and actions confirmed both your path to freedom and your baptismal mission—or revealed a detour you had inadvertently taken.

Spending ten to fifteen minutes every day with this or another examination of conscience will deepen your awareness of God's call and your response. It will help grow the grace of discernment.

Paragraph 166 of *Rejoice and Be Glad* mentions a third practice for the gift of discernment: *reading*. Scripture is essential because "listening entails obedience to the Gospel as the ultimate standard" (173). Reading, studying, and pondering the words and actions of Jesus strengthen our understanding of the seven principles of discernment, especially the seventh, dealing with the logic of the cross. "Very truly, I tell you, unless a grain of wheat falls into the earth and dies, it remains just a single grain; but if it dies, it bears much fruit" (John 12:24).

We are called to read and study the teachings of the Magisterium of the Church. The *Catholic Catechism* is a good place to start. There, "in the treasury of the Church," we find what is fruitful "for the 'today' of salvation" (173). It's in her Tradition that the Church receives and reveals the continuing revelation of God—a revelation that is priceless. Without the Church, we risk being poorer—and individualistic in our communal call to holiness.

Though the pontiff does not specifically mention it, let me add the importance of spiritual reading. Reading books about the spiritual life and spiritual formation gives us an awareness of the signposts and obstacles to look for as we discern the path to freedom; it also helps us absorb the wisdom of our spiritual tradition. Don't forget the lives of the beatified and canonized saints of our recent past. Searching the Web for their names and reading articles about these men and women not only remind us that holiness is a family affair, but also encourage each of us in discerning our own unique path to that holiness.

The final practice for the grace of discernment is *good counsel*. Discernment "calls for something more than intelligence or common sense" (166); though it includes reason and prudence, "it goes beyond them." This is where the wisdom and experience of spiritual directors or companions can be extraordinarily advantageous and beneficial. Don't be afraid to include people with "existential, psychological, sociological or moral insights drawn from the human sciences" —counselors, psychologists, medical doctors, and theologians. Their advice reminds us that God speaks to us through our own human experience—but know that discernment "transcends" (170) the facts they offer.

Discerning alone can get tricky—and so can seeking the counsel of clergy and religious. Pope Francis tells us that knowledge of the "Church's sound norms" is not "sufficient" (170). Writing about the need to listen to the Gospel and the Magisterium, he states emphatically: "It is not a matter of applying rules or repeating what was done in the past, since the same solutions are not valid in all circumstances and what was useful in one context may not prove so in another" (173). Discernment is a slippery slope, isn't it? Seeking wise counsel is imperative.

When is it necessary to discern?

The timing of discernment is crucial. Pope Francis highlights some important times when grace might be offered and our hearts are closed:

- when something new presents itself—the pope uses the word "novelty"—and we are challenged to decide "whether it is new wine brought by God or an illusion created by the spirit of this world or the spirit of the devil" (168);
- a time when we might rigidly resist change and have to examine "our desires, anxieties, fears and questions" while pondering "'the signs of the times'" (168);
- when we stand at a crossroads and "need to resolve grave problems and make crucial decisions" but also "in small and apparently irrelevant things" (169);
- a time when "God may be offering us something more, but in our comfortable inadvertence, we do not recognize it" (172).

Briefly, the pope encourages us to discern "at all times" (169).

All of this suggests that discernment is like a piece of software that is always operating in the background of our lives. We constantly listen to our lives, ponder our responses to circumstances and situations, and reflect on how we can give even more to God. I am reminded of the famous words of Socrates, uttered at his trial before he was sentenced to death: "The unexamined life is not worth living." The pope is calling us to adopt a reflective lifestyle.

What are the obstacles to discernment?

"Our desires, anxieties, fears and questions" (168) impede the walk to freedom and the discovery of our unique, baptismal mission. In practical terms, what do these obstacles and barriers look like?

"I have a good heart. I'm a decent person. I have the best of intentions." As a spiritual director, I have often heard this during spiritual direction sessions. Just yesterday, I myself said this to a retreatant who wanted to know if I thought I was going to heaven. But good intentions are not enough—the twelfth-century founder of the Cistercians, Bernard of Clairvaux, said, "Hell is full of good wishes or desires." Pope Francis writes, "Discernment also enables us to recognize the concrete means that the Lord provides in his mysterious and loving plan, to make us move beyond mere good intentions" (169). Intentions require action.

It's easy to equate a discerned direction in life with reason and prudence. "That sounds quite reasonable. You clearly have been moving in that direction. It makes perfect sense." But that's only part of the process—the seventeenth-century philosopher Blaise Pascal remarked, "The heart has its reasons which reason does not know." The pontiff reminds us that discernment, though including reason and prudence, goes beyond them, "for [discernment] seeks a glimpse of that unique and mysterious plan that God has for each of us, which takes shape amid so many varied situations and limitations" (170). Logic and discretion must surrender to mystery.

I have often thought that if I'm feeling peaceful and content and am satisfied with my accomplishments, I must be on the right path. After all, those feelings are a reward for doing God's will and being on the straight and narrow. The pope again surprises: "[Discernment] involves more than my temporal well-being, my satisfaction at having accomplished something useful, or even my desire for peace of mind." Always aiming for self-satisfaction can be a form of mediocrity and complacency, thus obstructing discernment's ultimate goal, which is "the real purpose of my life" (170).

The three obstacles mentioned—good intentions, reason and prudence, and a focus on feelings of well-being—can easily lead to rigidity. "We've always done it this way." "Don't upset the applecart." "If it ain't broke, don't fix it." Such attitudes snuff out the fire of the Spirit both in our individual lives and in community. "The discernment of spirits liberates us from rigidity, which has no place before the perennial 'today' of the risen Lord" (173).

Though rigidity has its roots in many desires, fears, and anxieties, Pope Francis implies two other roots. First, we are afraid to have our security shattered, and so we cling to our narrow-minded attitudes, the customs and habits we are used to, and our usual way of seeing things. This complacency hinders us from being led "to a better life" (172).

The second implied root of rigidity is our decision to shut the door of our hearts to grace and put up a sign that reads, "No Admittance." Or we leave a crack in the door to let the Spirit in "just so far." Pope Francis's wise advice is worth quoting in full:

When, in God's presence, we examine our life's journey, no areas can be off limits. In all aspects of life we can continue to grow and offer something greater to God, even in those areas we find most difficult. We need, though, to ask the Holy Spirit to liberate us and to expel the fear that makes us ban him from certain parts of our lives. God asks everything of us, yet he also gives everything to us. He does not want to enter our lives to cripple or diminish them, but to bring them to fulfilment. (175)

Mary as Model

The pope concludes his apostolic exhortation on holiness in the contemporary world by pointing us to the Virgin Mary. He shows how she is the embodiment of all that he has just discussed in *Gaudete et Exultate*: She lived the Beatitudes, which are the centerpiece of the pontiff's understanding of practical holiness. Rooted in God, she was a woman of joy. She discerned by listening, pondering, and treasuring everything in her heart. She wasn't afraid to sacrifice to the point of suffering. "Mary is the saint among the saints, blessed above all others" (176).

Rejoice and Be Glad is a blessing not only to Roman Catholics but also to all Orthodox and Protestant Christians—indeed, to anyone who is intentional about opening the door of the heart to grace, living the Beatitudes, and responding to God's call to holiness. In this simple document of one hundred seventy-seven paragraphs, Christians everywhere have the opportunity to read and reflect upon the wisdom of a wise spiritual companion who clearly promotes a piety that is pragmatic and practical. This is *Gaudete et Exsultate*'s contribution and challenge to the People of God.

The apostolic exhortation was signed at the Vatican on March 19, 2018, the Solemnity of Saint Joseph. Mary's husband was a great figure of obedience who never spoke a word in the Gospels. He simply opened the door of his heart to grace, followed his path to freedom, and fulfilled his God-given mission in the history of salvation. He's another example of Pope Francis's understanding of practical holiness.

REFLECTION QUESTIONS

1. What image best explains your understanding of the spiritual life? A battle? A relationship? Something else? Explain.

2. What comes to mind when you hear talk "of the devil"? How do you picture or imagine the devil to be?

3. What is the most reassuring aspect of discernment for you? The most challenging?

N ot everyone has the luxury of having a spiritual director or companion. Some of us live in faraway or out-of-the-way locations where spiritual direction is hard to find. Some of us have work schedules or homebound responsibilities that make seeing a spiritual director, or having a formal spiritual companion, inconvenient or even impossible. Thankfully, with *Rejoice and Be Glad*, we all have the opportunity to have a spiritual director who just so happens to be the pope. And his approach to holiness is eminently practical.

Pope Francis challenges and encourages us to find our own unique path to holiness—we're not meant to playact the life of a favorite saint. Like Jesus, the Word made flesh, each one of us is a word that God deliberately chooses to speak to the world. And like Jesus, each one of us is called to enflesh love in both heroic and ordinary ways. How we uniquely do that is the secret to our sanctity.

Our holiness is not betrayed by hifalutin thoughts or esoteric experiences. Nor is there a self-service checkout lane to acquire it. How do we know if the process of spiritual transformation is occurring within us? The door of the heart is open to grace and joyfully brims over with tenacious love for others.

Love *is* holiness. It is the highest expression of our worship of God and the practical measure of our love for God. It validates the authenticity of our prayer life. It opens our eyes to the vision of God enfleshed in our suffering brothers and sisters.

Discerning the ways we get lost on the spiritual journey is important. We constantly need to be on the lookout for the lies presented to us by the ego, the digital age, the mentality of the world, our weaknesses and sinful inclinations, and the seductions of the devil.

Pope Francis ultimately assures us that the call to holiness is a family affair—we *need* our spouses, children, friends, and relatives as well as the holy people and canonized saints who have gone before us. Their encouragement and example help us not only to live the Beatitudes, the centerpiece of the pontiff's understanding of practical holiness, but also to practice the works of mercy. Closing the door of the heart to others is closing it to grace.

What's Next?

Perhaps you have been both challenged and consoled by Pope Francis's understanding of practical holiness. Now you want to explore its implication for your own life. Or maybe this book and the apostolic exhortation have piqued your interest in the search for a spiritual director. How do you find one?

Start by contacting your local church. Some have a list of spiritual directors or companions in the parish or the area. If you know a priest, religious sister, or a lay person whose spiritual life attracts you, ask if he or she might be willing to meet with you on a monthly or bi-monthly basis to discuss what God is doing in your life.

Consider inquiring at nearby convents, monasteries, retreat houses, or Christian conference centers. Many offer spiritual direction as an outreach to the wider Christian community.

Don't hesitate mentioning your interest in finding a spiritual companion to family and friends. You'll be surprised when someone says, "I hear Father So-and-so or Sister So-and-so does spiritual direction." Don't be surprised if you hear the names of lay people, because many have been trained in the art of spiritual direction.

If you're still having difficulty finding a spiritual director or companion, visit the website for Spiritual Directors International, www.SDIworld.org. Click on the "Seek and Find Guide." Spend time reading the articles on the left-hand side of the screen. Pay particular attention to the articles entitled "Spiritual Direction 101," "Misconceptions about Spiritual Direction," and "Questions to ask a potential SD."

"Spiritual Direction 101" will introduce you to some helpful vocabulary. You'll also find some short video clips highlighting the benefits of having a spiritual director.

"Misconceptions about Spiritual Direction" might address some of your concerns and hesitation.

Fill out the "Seek and Find" form in the center of the screen. Click on *submit* and notice the names and contact information for spiritual directors in the geographical area you selected. This is a free resource.

Spend time pondering whether or not God is calling you to choose a spiritual director or companion to help keep you grounded in Pope Francis's call to practical holiness. If the answer is yes, contact two or three potential spiritual directors and interview each. You'll find some helpful questions to ask in "Questions to ask a potential SD."

If you feel a connection with one of the people you have interviewed, commit to a few spiritual direction sessions—four is a good start. Afterward, reassess the help and usefulness for you.

What do you talk about during a spiritual direction session? A good place to start the conversation is to bring the answers to these questions:

- What is God up to in my life these days?
- How am I being consoled by God?
- How am I being stretched and challenged by God in the circumstances of my life and my relationships?
- What am I discovering as I pray over my life?
- How do I see myself helping Jesus build the kingdom of justice, peace, and love?
- What mission has God given me to accomplish?
- What is the word that God wants to speak through me?

If you are hesitant for a one-on-one relationship with a spiritual director or companion, consider starting a spiritual direction group. A spiritual direction group consists of four to eight people who periodically come together to explore and discuss their spiritual lives. More than faith sharing, this discussion and exploration help each person in the group to understand more deeply their unique mission. Alice Fryling's *Seeking God Together: An Introduction to Group Spiritual Direction* (Downers Grove, IL: InterVarsity Press, 2009) is an excellent resource that offers practical tips for forming, running, and managing spiritual direction groups.

The practical holiness envisioned by Pope Francis doesn't happen by osmosis. And, as he reminds us in the apostolic exhortation, it doesn't happen alone. It requires both a commitment and a companion. Spiritual direction offers both.

Forty Questions for Forty Days

The number forty has a biblical resonance. It rained for forty days and forty nights at the time of Noah (Gen. 7:12). Moses spent forty days and forty nights on Mount Sinai (Exod. 24:18) and interceded on Israel's behalf for forty days and forty nights (Deut. 9:18, 25). When Elijah fled from Jezebel, he wandered forty days and forty nights to Mount Horeb (1 Kgs. 19:8). Jonah gave the people of Nineveh forty days to repent or be destroyed (Jonah 3:4). Jesus was tempted in the desert for forty days and forty nights (Matt. 4:2). There were forty days between Jesus's resurrection and ascension (Acts 1:3).

No doubt influenced by these scriptural references, the early Church, already by the end of the fourth century, began noting the apostolic origins of the forty days of Lent. Lent was a time for Christians to pray, fast, and give alms—and recommit themselves to the following of Christ.

In this spirit, I offer the following forty reflection questions based upon *Gaudete et Exsultate*. The concluding number(s) in parentheses refers to the text's specific paragraph(s) that elicited the question.

You might want to spend the forty days of Lent—or any period of forty consecutive days—with one question per day. This would be a practical way to remind and recommit yourself to the practical holiness called for by Pope Francis.

You might want to survey and reflect upon all the questions from one chapter of the apostolic exhortation. Bring your reflections to your spiritual companion and explore the practical implications of that chapter on your life.

Start a five-session study group centered upon *Rejoice and Be Glad: On the Call to Holiness in Today's World*. Each week focus on one chapter of the apostolic exhortation and ask each participant to bring the answers to these questions to the session. This will result in a depth of faith sharing that could be both challenging and consoling.

Incorporate the five-session study group as part of the Mystagogia of your Rite of Christian Initiation of Adults (RCIA) program.

If you don't have a spiritual companion, you can still use these questions as reminders of the practical holiness your "literary" spiritual director, Pope Francis, asks you to consider.

The Call to Holiness

1. Whom do you consider belonging to "the middle class of holiness" among your family, friends, and acquaintances? Why? (7)

2. What specific path of holiness has God called you to walk? How do you know it's your path? (11)

3. Name some feminine styles of holiness that you have witnessed. How did they challenge or encourage you? (12)

4. What various aspects of Jesus's earthly life do you reproduce in your own life? How are your choices and attitudes affected by them? Be specific. (20)

5. What word or message of Jesus does God want to speak to the world through you? How conscious are you of it in daily life? (24)

6. In what practical ways do you build with Jesus the kingdom of love, justice, and universal peace? Be specific. (25)

7. When are you tempted "to love silence while fleeing interaction with others, to want peace and quiet while avoiding activity, to seek prayer while disdaining service"? How do you typically resolve that tension? (26)

8. How does fear paralyze you from setting your sights higher and allowing yourself to be loved and liberated by God? What fears hinder you from following the lead of the Holy Spirit? (34)

Two Subtle Enemies of Holiness

9. In what ways have you made the Gospel comprehensible and reduced Jesus's teachings "to a cold and harsh logic that seeks to dominate everything"? (39)

10. How is God a mystery to you? How have your thoughts, theories, religious knowledge, and spiritual vision domesticated the mystery of God? (40)

11. What person or groups of people, because of their choices or lifestyle, are abandoned by God? How can they find salvation? (42)

12. When and how often do you trust in your own strength and will power to overcome weakness, temptation, and sin? How successful have you been with overcoming them on your own? (49)

13. Reflect on your life. How have you progressively grown in holiness? Who and what made it possible? Explain. (50)

14. How much time and energy do you expend on "an obsession with the law, an absorption with social and political advantages, a punctilious concern for the Church's liturgy, doctrine and prestige, a vanity about the ability to manage practical matters, and an excessive concern with programs of self-help and personal fulfilment"? What comfort do you derive from these thoughts and actions? On what rules, customs, and

ways of acting do you place excessive importance? (57–58)

15. In what practical ways do you see the face of God reflected in the least, the most vulnerable, the defenseless, and those in need? (61)

In the Light of the Master

16. Reflect on Matthew's version of the Beatitudes (Matt. 6:3–12). How do your weaknesses, selfishness, complacency, and pride hinder you from living them? (65)

17. Reflect on the parable of the Judgment of the Nations (Matt. 25:31–46). Where do you see yourself in this parable? (95–96)

18. What race, color, creed, or lifestyle do you struggle to accept? Can you respond to such people with faith and charity, seeing in each individual "a human being with a dignity identical to my own, a creature infinitely loved by the Father, an image of God, a brother or sister redeemed by Jesus Christ"? In what practical ways can you work for social change for these people? (98–99)

19. When have you so overemphasized the commitment to work for peace and social justice that it was separated from your personal relationship with the Lord? When have you so overemphasized your prayer and personal relationship with the Lord that you viewed your social

engagement with others as superficial, worldly, secular, or materialist? (100–101)

20. What's your opinion about immigrants, migrants, and the undocumented? (102–103)

21. "Those who really wish to give glory to God by their lives, who truly long to grow in holiness, are called to be single-minded and tenacious in their practice of the works of mercy." What works of mercy do you practice on a regular basis? How can you grow your enthusiasm for practicing works of mercy? (107)

Signs of Holiness in Today's World

22. Do you have a solid grounding in God? Under what circumstances does it waiver? How does it inform your perseverance, patience, and meekness? (112)

23. When have you been caught up in verbal violence promoted by the Web and various means of digital communication? When have you violated the eighth commandment? Be specific. (115)

24. In what situations are you prone to judge others, complain about them, or look down upon them? (116–117)

25. What humiliations have you endured? How did you accept them? How did they bring you closer to Jesus or keep you farther away from him? Explain. (118–120)

26. On a scale of 1 (living with timidity, sarcasm, or melancholy) to 4 (living with joy and a sense of humor),

where would you place yourself? What worries and anxieties weigh you down? (122)

27. How strong and bold is your sense of mission? What fears keep you from speaking the truth? (129–133)

28. How have individualism, spiritualism, living in a little world, addiction, intransigence, the rejection of new ideas and approaches, dogmatism, nostalgia, pessimism, or hiding behind rules and regulations kept you entrenched in the familiar and easy way of doing things? How have they hindered you from following the call of the Spirit? (134)

29. How does your "stale self-centeredness" keep Jesus a prisoner of your heart? (136)

30. Because holiness is a journey in community, who are your companions on the spiritual journey? How do they challenge and encourage you? (141)

31. When did you share a profound spiritual experience with someone else? How did that experience affect you and your relationship with the other person? (142–143)

32. When have you been the recipient of "the small details of love"? How have you been attentive and offered love in the small details of everyday life? (144–145)

33. How has your prayer life helped you to discover your unique path to holiness? (150)

34. How do you understand the prayers of supplication, petition, and intercession? What roles, if any, do they play in your daily prayer? (154)

Spiritual Combat, Vigilance, and Discernment

35. What has been your experience with the devil and the powers of evil? How would you describe Satan? (160–161)

36. What spiritual resources keep you vigilant in your struggle against the devil? (162–164)

37. How do you develop the gift of discernment in your spiritual life? (166)

38. Name a time in your life when a discerned decision, clearly going beyond reason and prudence, made no sense and perhaps made you look foolish. What fears, doubts, and concerns did the decision raise? What was the outcome after your discernment and decision? (170)

39. In what practical ways does God speak to you "at work, through others and at every moment"? How do you know it is God who is speaking and not your imagination? (171)

40. How do you experience the "logic" of the cross in your life? In what areas of your life do you refuse God admittance? (174–175)

ABOUT PARACLETE PRESS

Who We Are

As the publishing arm of the Community of Jesus, Paraclete Press presents a full expression of Christian belief and practice—from Catholic to Evangelical, from Protestant to Orthodox, reflecting the ecumenical charism of the Community and its dedication to sacred music, the fine arts, and the written word. We publish books, recordings, sheet music, and video/DVDs that nourish the vibrant life of the church and its people.

What We Are Doing

BOOKS

PARACLETE PRESS BOOKS show the richness and depth of what it means to be Christian. While Benedictine spirituality is at the heart of who we are and all that we do, our books reflect the Christian experience across many cultures, time periods, and houses of worship.

We have many series, including *Paraclete Essentials*; *Paraclete Fiction*; *Paraclete Poetry*; *Paraclete Giants*; and for children and adults, *All God's Creatures*, books about animals and faith; and *San Damiano Books*, focusing on Franciscan spirituality. Others include *Voices from the Monastery* (men and women monastics writing about living a spiritual life today), *Active Prayer*, and new for young readers: *The Pope's Cat*. We also specialize in gift books for children on the occasions of Baptism and First Communion, as well as other important times in a child's life, and books that bring creativity and liveliness to any adult spiritual life.

The MOUNT TABOR BOOKS series focuses on the arts and literature as well as liturgical worship and spirituality; it was created in conjunction with the Mount Tabor Ecumenical Centre for Art and Spirituality in Barga, Italy.

MUSIC

The PARACLETE RECORDINGS label represents the internationally acclaimed choir *Gloriæ Dei Cantores*, the *Gloriæ Dei Cantores Schola*, and the other instrumental artists of the *Arts Empowering Life Foundation*.

Paraclete Press is the exclusive North American distributor for the Gregorian chant recordings from St. Peter's Abbey in Solesmes, France. Paraclete also carries all of the Solesmes chant publications for Mass and the Divine Office, as well as their academic research publications.

In addition, PARACLETE PRESS SHEET MUSIC publishes the work of today's finest composers of sacred choral music, annually reviewing over 1,000 works and releasing between 40 and 60 works for both choir and organ.

VIDEO

Our video/DVDs offer spiritual help, healing, and biblical guidance for a broad range of life issues including grief and loss, marriage, forgiveness, facing death, understanding suicide, bullying, addictions, Alzheimer's, and Christian formation.

Learn more about us at our website
www.paracletepress.com
or phone us toll-free at 1.800.451.5006

SCAN TO READ MORE